SCHOOLS FOR ALL LEARNERS:
BEYOND THE BELL CURVE

Renfro C. Manning

Superintendent
Orange County School District

EYE ON EDUCATION
P.O. BOX 388
PRINCETON JUNCTION, NJ 08550
(609) 799-9188
(609) 799-3698 fax

Editorial and production services provided by Richard H. Adin Freelance Editorial Services, 9 Orchard Drive, Gardiner, NY 12525 (914-883-5884)

ISBN 1-883001-06-4

Library of Congress Cataloging-in-Publication Data

Manning, Renfro C.
  Schools for all learners: beyond the bell curve / by Renfro C. Manning.
      p. cm.
  Includes bibliographical references and index.
  ISBN 1-883001-06-4
  1. School management and organization—United States. 2. School supervision—United States. 3. School improvement programs—United States. 4. Public schools—United States—Aims and objectives.
I. Title.
LB2805.M277 1994
371.2'00973—dc20   94-34139
                                                                CIP

Printing 9 8 7 6 5 4 3 2 1

DEDICATION

This book is dedicated to those who perceive the need to change public education. It is also dedicated to those who recognize that even with the great accomplishments of public education there is now a necessity to move forward to a new plateau, to a model designed around success for all students.

Special acknowledgement is given to the many colleagues—too numerous to mention, but appreciated nonetheless—who have offered suggestions, ideas, and criticism. Specifically, two individuals motivated chapters in this book. Chapter 7, Moral and Ethical Considerations, was written as I recalled the words of Dr. William Hunter Seawell, who was Chairman of the Department of Administration and Supervision at the University of Virginia. He had the ability to subtly weave into his lectures the moral and ethical aspects of each topic he discussed. To him, education was an exercise in ethical responsibility.

As I watched my own son, William Clark Manning, matriculate through school, I began to understand the value of student activities and how they related inseparably to academic achievement. Chapter 4 is his chapter.

Finally, Mrs. Rosa F. Anderson, executive secretary and colleague for many years, typed, critiqued, and at times "fumed" until the manuscript was finished. Her assistance, as always, was invaluable.

TABLE OF CONTENTS

ABOUT THE AUTHOR

Renfro Manning, EdD., University of Virginia, is the Superintendent of Schools in Orange County, Virginia, a system nationally known for its effective, innovative programs. Past President of the Virginia Association of School Superintendents, Dr. Manning is the author of *The Teacher Evaluation Handbook* (Prentice-Hall). He has taught various graduate courses covering a wide range of educational topics.

INTRODUCTION

Schools for All Learners: Beyond the Bell Curve is about improving the schools. It is written with the belief that we must move beyond the bell curve in order to permit vast numbers of students to become successful learners. The bell curve symbolically represents the select and sort model of education which emerged with the industrial revolution—it is now obsolete.

The view of education which supports the select and sort process assumes that only a limited number of students can learn well; and it relegates slower learners to groups in which they can "have their needs met." It also props up a vast norm-referenced testing industry which thrives on public education.

The bell curve model covers contemporary education like a large net. This net creates boundaries which limit the effectiveness of grading, grouping, teacher evaluation, visioning, goal setting, and student activities. It also serves to protect insiders from outside intrusion. Therefore, in order for real change to occur, schools must move beyond the bell curve.

A move to a new model must be built on the optimistic premise that all, or at least most, students can and should learn that which we propose to teach. This must be accomplished by involving the constituency of education in a collegial process which builds a consensus concerning needed changes.

Moving beyond the bell curve is accomplished by examining every practice in education, ensuring each is designed to support student success. Most current practices in education evolved with the support of the select and sort model. Therefore, we must examine each practice and ask the question, "How would this look if we were expecting success for all learners?" An approach to change in a less comprehensive manner leads to tinkering which does not produce significant or lasting results as was shown in the failed reforms of the '80s and early '90s.

In *Schools for All Learners: Beyond the Bell Curve*, I examine many of the primary components of education. The word component no longer means any item or practice changed in isolation with little impact upon the whole. Once systemwide (contextual) change becomes the goal, components are key parts aligned to the new model. It is the goal of this book to assist educators to view education differently and to move Beyond the Bell Curve.

1

TAKING EDUCATION BEYOND THE BELL CURVE

INTRODUCTION

The school reform movement is filled with paradoxes. For example, there is a call for increased standards and, at the same time, a demand to reduce dropouts. In fact, to simply increase standards without attending to the special needs of a large number of students will increase dropouts. There is a movement toward local school autonomy, but mandates from the top down continue. There is strong advocacy for all children to learn, but continued support of homogeneous grouping. Of course, there are many other contradictions in education, perhaps, too many to count. In the face of this inconsistency, the central question is: what is real change and what is tinkering?

Educational reformers come from diverse and varied backgrounds. They may be teachers, parents, politicians, school administrators from all levels, school board members, and others. Therefore, by necessity, the intended audience of this book is quite broad. Educational leaders, especially principals and other administrators who must advocate and support reform, will find the ideas included to be quite helpful. This chapter also explains why many of the first and second wave reform efforts have had little impact. Those who would reform education must analyze carefully which factors will help schools move beyond the bell curve and make schools a better place for students.

THE REFORM MOVEMENT EMERGES

During the early '80s, there emerged a broad consensus that the public schools were not functioning properly. There were literally dozens of reports outlining the problems of public education. Most reports, even the one published by the federal government, did not correctly interpret what had happened within society or what would be required to properly align education with the needs of society. In fact, *most* studies and reports called for more of the same (more classes, more time, and more training for teachers) to solve a problem only partially identified. Of course, more of the same contributed little to changing a model which was not producing the desired result. If nothing else, these reports helped educators realize that there was widespread frustration with public education.

As political and business leaders realized there was a problem with public education, it was quite naturally viewed as one of productivity. Some leaders knew that problems with international economic competitiveness could not be placed at the schoolhouse door, but the schools made a good target. It was easier to blame schools than address profound social and economic problems.

Now, with a little hindsight and the help of astute observers like Glen Robinson of the Educational Research Service, it has become clear that the productivity of public education was not the primary problem. The very *mission* of public education was out of sync with the needs and expectancies of society.

In reality, schools were succeeding (with the exception of a few urban centers where all institutions had virtually disintegrated), but for the wrong purpose. The dissatisfaction with public education was due to an obsolete mission which allowed too many students to be programmed as slow learners. For these slow learners, school became unchallenging and "lock step." Many of these students became dropouts, viewed as having a high potential to become serious and long-term problems for society.

Figure 1.1 will assist in understanding the mission change

which is now broadly affecting education (1).

FIGURE 1.1 THE MISSION OF EDUCATION

Era One—Some education for many
Era Two—Much education for a few
Era Three—Much education for many

NOTES:

In Era One, it was important to have a literate society. This was desired to preserve democracy and for the basic needs of successful living. This era had its beginning with the first public schools and lasted until the industrial revolution was well underway.

In Era Two, the country was in the industrial revolution, and the mission of education was to select and sort in order to produce workers and a few leaders. The end of this era occurred during the decade of the '70s. The bell curve of human variability was developed in this era.

In Era Three, the needs for marginally educated industrial workers declined, and the age of technology began. There were limited opportunities for the undereducated because the workplace required greater skills. Society could no longer afford the select and sort mission. A new mission began to emerge—much education for many, and success for all learners. A "skewed" curve now represents the learning expectancy.

(Adapted from Glen E. Robinson, *Learning Expectancy, A Force Changing Education*, Arlington, VA 22209: Educational Research Service, February 1986.)

THE FIASCO WITH NORM REFERENCED TESTS— A TOOL OF THE BELL-SHAPED CURVE

Frequently, when productivity of the public schools is questioned, the decline in Scholastic Aptitude Test (S.A.T.) scores and other norm referenced tests are used to indict both elementary and secondary schools. The problem with the S.A.T. scores is an almost perfect example of how the mission of public education has changed, but the public mistakenly assumes a problem with the productivity of public education.

During the first half of the 20th Century, the function of education was to "select and sort." The bell-shaped curve was utilized as a vehicle to lend statistical credibility to this selecting and sorting process. Norm referenced tests were created to place students in their respective places on the bell-shaped curve. During this period, the system broadly recognized that some students could finish elementary school, some could graduate from high school, and a few could go to college. The expectation was that many students would drop out of school, and there was plenty of need for the resulting labor pool in factories and on the farms. The Scholastic Aptitude Test (S.A.T.) became a norm referenced test used to identify the students for college entrance.

During the last two generations, society changed, and a need grew for more people with higher levels of education. The number of students who sought higher education increased. A very select group originally took the S.A.T., but this group has become less homogeneous. Because of this larger group, test scores declined slightly. This caused a raft of negative publicity for the schools. In order to properly assess whether or not the S.A.T. scores have actually declined, the present population of test takers would have to be reduced by selective factors to equal those who took the test several years ago.

What would be the result of research corrected for the difference in test-taking populations? Today's scores on the S.A.T. would, in fact, be higher than in the past. The decline in scores is not real, and, therefore, the test is not a valid indicator of decline in student learning. The entire S.A.T. fiasco results from taking methodology used during the "selecting and sorting era" and applying it to a vastly changed population and a society which expects a much larger number of students to meet a higher level of success.

The S.A.T. is being revised, and this revision will reflect the changes in the test-taking population to some extent. However, it will continue to be an instrument in support of the "select and sort" model. The mission for schools has changed, and success will be perceived only when *all* takers of the test score higher than the previously selective group.

The idea of learning for all will flow into a natural harbor—opportunity for all. If reform efforts align schools with the new needs of society, the S.A.T. will come under increasing pressure.

Selecting out students on the basis of a test which cannot adequately measure potential for the diverse student population now seeking college admission will not be tolerated. As the movement toward authentic assessment grows, it is predicted that colleges will begin looking for demonstrable skills.

In addition to being a tool for the select and sort, bell-curve model, standardized tests are used to judge educational quality. Norm referenced tests are one of the most significant inhibitors of real change in education. Glasser contended that nothing of quality can be measured by standard machine scored tests (2). Yet, standardized tests are a favored tool of many failed school reform efforts.

If schools are to teach significant outcomes such as problem solving skills, cooperative effort, and higher level thinking skills, other means of accountability must be developed. Further, those who develop standardized multiple choice tests have real difficulty in measuring work ethic, task commitment, and technological literacy, all identified as extremely important by those in business and industry.

Reformers may never be able to completely eliminate standardized tests. This issue has too much political baggage. The successful reformer must decide how to address the needs of standardized testing while proceeding with other meaningful assessment. Standardized tests must not be allowed to drive the curriculum.

One reason standardized tests are cited as a barrier to reform is that they generally require the ability to recall somewhat unrelated facts. Test scores can be raised by drill and practice—drill and practice of the skills identified by the test writers. To maintain credibility, public school educators, particularly those with large enrollments of at risk students, must take class time for drill and practice. It's interesting that drill and practice is directed toward having students "cough up" facts without engaging in the kind of applicational thinking that school critics demand. One merchant employed a very bright student as a summer part-time employee and later criticized the schools because the student had to be taught how to count change. Of course, the student quickly learned this skill, but this example depicts just the tip of the iceberg concerning the need for application and analytical skills.

Once a school system decides upon a reform agenda and moves toward assuring success for all students, a new and different kind of assessment becomes important. Assessment becomes continual, and it is usually accomplished with criterion-referenced techniques. Teachers soon recognize that standardized testing is a regression to the select and sort model. All of this may cause a slight decline in standardized test scores.

The decline in test scores, if there is one, should be only slight and only for a year or two. The problem comes when the "nay-sayers" seize upon this as a reason to advocate a return to the old model. But remember, with the old model we must expect and force many students into the lower half of the bell curve.

Any considerations of issues about the productivity of America's schools would be incomplete without the analysis offered by Schneider and Houston. They recognize that the challenge is to surpass the select and sort model. They also say that political expediency has created the need to make public education appear worse—much worse—than the data supports.

> "For example, the more we peeled away the rhetoric encasing federal and corporate-backed educational reform initiatives, the more we found the logic and agenda of a handful of neoconservatives who are openly hostile to the common school and its efforts to educate everyone, regardless of circumstances. By embracing the argument advanced by politicians and business leaders that schools are to blame for poorly trained workers, who in turn are the reason the economy is in the toilet, the neoconservatives have gained a cloak of respectability for their sort'em-and-flunk'em approach to education. Working in tandem, political, business, and neoconservative leaders have produced a federal crusade to reform schools. Having wrapped it in red, white, and blue bunting, they call it AMERICA 2000. It's stated aim is to reform schools; its real objective, though, is twofold. One is to keep the public from focusing on the real

tough economic issues facing our country and the work-place. The second is to use public funds to support private schools through parental-choice programs." (3)

It is true that public education is much better than generally recognized. It is also apparent that those with a vested interest have contributed greatly to the misperception that the public schools are not productive. But, as stated elsewhere, the present model of education is giving results which are about as good as can be expected for this model. As expectancy has changed, so must the model of education change. Educational reformers must look at ways of doing business which will permit success for a much greater number of students.

ALIGNMENT

The reform movement has resulted in recognition of the misalignment between education and the new needs of society. An examination of the various reform thrusts—restructuring the schools, empowerment of teachers, site-based management, outcome-based education, the quality movement, and others—reveals that one common goal reflects the needs of society—increasing the number of successful students. However, attempting to increase the number of successful students while paying homage to the bell curve model is unethical.

Calling for success for more students arouses the fear that the curriculum will be "watered down." "Dumbing down" the curriculum will result in a disservice to students. The call for more success means that a larger number of students should learn effectively meaningful standards or outcomes of significance. (Later, this will be identified as complete learning for a larger number of students.)

Understanding that the push for educational reform comes primarily from a need to change the mission leads to some clear implications for school reforms. The first and foremost implication is that society will not continue to support a school operation which produces low-level learners, as an expectancy. Lower level learners were not considered dysfunctional or a societal liability a generation ago—at least, not like the present. We now know that lower level learners are dysfunctional. They constitute an intolerable liability to society. The overwhelming problems of society make the mission change even more critical. Kearns and Doyle cited the problems of society as creating an even greater challenge to those who would improve our schools as follows:

> "In fact, the bleak lives of disadvantaged and dispossessed children is a compelling argument for making school restructuring a priority. For a lot of youngsters, the only good thing that happens to them happens at school—a teacher's smile, the feeling of accomplishment when they master a math problem, the excitement of going on a field trip.
>
> If we can make our schools better, we'll have a better chance to help those children lead useful, productive, happier lives. Shifting the focus away from changing our schools only means deferring change, letting the problems sink deeper, defeating the hopes of the generation of students now in our classrooms. Our deep social problems cannot become an excuse for the school's failures. They should be a spur to change the system to better serve the victims of those problems." (4)

TINKERING

A member of a state legislature recently said to me:

> "This school reform business is paying very small dividends. We have literally spent millions of dollars during the last five or six years, and our schools have changed very little."

> "What do you think is the reason for this?" I asked.

Of course, the reply was not surprising.

> "That's the sixty-four thousand dollar question! The test scores aren't much better, the dropout rate is still too high, violence is prevalent. It's as if all of our efforts are ignored by the education establishment."

Further questioning would have produced other predictable answers. For example, asking what should be done next would have produced answers such as choice, charter schools, more mandates, site-based management, etc. There would be three predictable characteristics of the proposed solutions:

- ◆ They would tend to follow political party lines.
- ◆ Solutions would be unproven and postulated without thought for research or unintended side effects.
- ◆ They would aim to protect the public from the education establishment.

Why does little seem to be working in so many places? —*Because most changes are nothing more than tinkering.* A look at just a few of the changes occurring in various localities throughout the nation might be revealing—

- ◆ Reduce pupil/teacher ratio
- ◆ Increase teacher salaries
- ◆ Provide free textbooks
- ◆ Increase the state testing program
- ◆ Require elementary guidance
- ◆ Create statewide accountability measures
- ◆ Increase expenditures for teacher training
- ◆ Require teacher strength evaluations
- ◆ Adopt measures for equalized funding
- ◆ Add class requirements (*e.g.*, Alabama now requires four credits each in math, science, social studies, and English).

The items listed are typical of actions which have been legislated in many states. Educators would agree with the value of most, but it is obvious that none relate to a mission change or to going beyond the bell curve. They are simply tinkering with the existing model.

Contextual change is required to move schooling from a model which anticipates little success for almost half the students. Education must now expect much success for all and exceptional success for some.

Those who are familiar with organizational research will

recognize the term "contextual" as implying second order change (5). First order change does not challenge the underlying assumptions of an organization; second order change does.

To change underlying assumptions is literally to change the culture of the organization. Change of this magnitude is likely to be unsettling at the very least. It can be time consuming and "all consuming."

Tinkering is defined as change to support or strengthen the existing model. All 10 of the typical changes listed above are directed toward improving the existing model. This is the primary reason that school reform activities have had little impact or why they may have even been counterproductive? We must abandon the consideration of tinkering as a means of change for the existing model of education. It is now time to look toward contextual change.

CONTEXTUAL CHANGE

Many of the first order change components are excellent ways to strengthen the existing model. As such, they may be more useful than no change at all; but real progress requires contextual change. It must be recognized that changes in the needs of society have thrust education into a new era. Thoughtful critics of education contend that the present education system is unworkable, they don't disdain public education, but they recognize the limitations of the existing model.

Other critics do not explain or, perhaps, understand the ramifications of that which they are advocating. This is the reason many make the mistaken assumption that a new direction can be created with additional or parallel institutions, thus the advocacy for charter schools and choice. Actually, these proposals are nothing more than higher order "tinkering."

To charter schools or to support private education with public vouchers will not guarantee a move away from the select and sort model or the bell-shaped curve as a cognitive model. In fact, some of the most ardent adherents for the old model of education can be found among the private schools. Many times private schools serve a clientele which has already been selected. Even then much success for all is not an expectancy and the bell curve frequently is used for grading.

The most productive way to create a new institution is to transform the existing institution through properly directed reform or restructuring. There is even a problem with this method. How can an institution deeply ingrained in the old model change its very nature? It's difficult, but not impossible, to restructure an organization. Good examples are emerging frequently.

There are no proven techniques for bringing about contextual change, no prescriptions, and no "sure fire" solutions. There are, however, some guidelines from those who have succeeded. Actions recognized as generally helpful in initiating change will serve as productive models. Then, there are those who oppose any change. They are the "gatekeepers." Some advice exists about how to defend the school from the onslaught of "gatekeepers" who will oppose any change.

The "gatekeepers" are those who are comfortable in the existing reality. The status quo meets many important needs, such as power, achievement (at least a modest level), and even survival. Some people are reluctant to embark on a new course that could jeopardize this. They will "what if" a new proposal into oblivion. (We discuss ways to work with this "what if" obstacle in the chapter on administering the new organization.)

SOME BASICS FOR REFORM

The first actions for school reformers who wish to succeed is to show others who must be involved how change can fulfill needs. This makes the involvement of existing "stakeholders" extremely critical. They must be formed into committees, study groups, and must even become leaders in the new effort. In seeking second order change, tending to the disaffected, those who initially feel threatened due to a sense of loss, is critical. All reform efforts will be resisted or "watered down" to make them first order unless the needs of the disaffected are met.

Here it is valuable to consider Glasser's characterization of needs—love, power, survival, fun, and freedom (6). These needs drive human motivation; it's somewhat threatening to consider change. In the existing school structure (the one which supports the bell-shaped curve), there are many competent people who are perfectly comfortable. They understand the system. They may be dissatisfied with its results, but it provides for some need fulfillment. Typically, they believe its problems can be fixed by innovation or by just working harder.

These persons—teachers, administrators, and others—will gravitate "back to the future" as soon as a contextual change creates discomfort. Changing a culture which has fulfilled any needs is discomforting. There are complicated cultural relationships in the old structure, and second order change will quickly cause disequilibrium.

The disequilibrium created in Kentucky as the result of a school reform model has been interesting to observe. The legislative action creating reform was initiated as a result of an equity of funding suit. The Kentucky experiment is a top-down effort to reform education and local governance as well.

Initially, more state funds were pumped into education, and the Kentucky reform act received broad acceptance. But as changes disrupted local culture, significant resistance began to build. *Education Week* reported the cultural disruption created by Kentucky's landmark education reform law: "While many have welcomed the new system, in recent months the state has found itself in a contest of political hardball against local officials determined to protect both their personal prerogatives and their regional independence" (7).

As resistance builds in Kentucky, it is now questionable if the state can stay the course. As elections are conducted, the critics of change may gain some significant seats in the legislature. The primary hope for Kentucky is that localities outside of Eastern Kentucky, where resistance is greatest, will continue to support reform.

It's amazing that the paradigm change in Kentucky does not appear to involve education as much as politics. The education reform involves many first order innovations. The contextual part of reform has been directed toward reforming the political system which was viewed as preventing educational change. Conflict arose from efforts to reform nepotism, management, and local authority. This makes the author, who is originally from Kentucky, wonder—aren't they arguing about the wrong things? Has contextual change in politics become the focus rather than the contextual change in education which was desired? The point is, any part of a reform movement which involves contextual change will create discomfort and it must be addressed if change is to survive.

One outcome of contextual or second order change is persons working within the organization feel discomfort. In order for a new paradigm to survive, a host of need-fulfilling opportunities must exist and be made very apparent. Need-fulfilling activities may be training, responsibility, or collaboration. These activities are often mistaken as change. This is not true. They are simply first level components. In need fulfillment, money and resources are helpful, but they are not the most important items.

Some other examples of the first level components are teacher empowerment, site-based management, implementation committees, inservice opportunities, study groups, school climate efforts, and even the quality movement. Deming's work on quality may cause its adherents to back into a new paradigm by its very emphasis on quality. However, if the bell-shaped curve model continues, Deming's work could create an effective organization only within these parameters. As we discussed, an effective organization with an obsolete mission will not produce the desired result.

All first level components will be of value if their use is in helping the existing culture to adopt a new paradigm—"every student a successful learner" and no "bell-shaped mentality."

If "Success For All" is to be adopted with passion, the very concept which this represents will force moving beyond the bell curve. This is true because the concept of all students becoming successful learners is simply not a part of the paradigm of the old model for education. Levine and Ornstein made the following observation about success for a program which applies to the school effectiveness movement:

> "Probably the most comprehensive intervention to raise achievement of disadvantaged students, Success For All, gives intensive instructional support and family assistance to children in preschool and the primary grades. The curriculum and instruction emphasize language and learning to learn skills and provide help to individual students in small classes.

Other elements of the program include cooperative learning, in which students work and learn together, and mastery instruction, in which teachers give frequent assessments to find out whether students have mastered material before moving on. The program also includes technical support and staff development for teachers delivered by full-time consultative and resource people assigned to schools. The developers of Success For All have described its early results as supporting the conclusion that nearly all students can learn well—beginning at the earliest grades—and, therefore, can avoid placement in remedial classes or special education" (8).

It should be clear by now that a mission of "Success For All" is far more than just a empty slogan, but is, in fact, the concept which leads to many actions supporting contextual change.

A DIAGRAM OF CHANGE

Now that some of the terms of change have been used, how would this process appear if diagrammed? Is there a hierarchy of events? Various writers disagree, but Figure 1.2 is a compilation.

There is some speculation as to whether a mission is the defining of purpose in support of the vision or whether the vision is developed once the mission is decided. At any rate, the vision projects where we want to be in the future, and the mission defines what our business is about.

The vision of an organization could become quite lengthy because it is a statement about the organizational future. In education, those with a stake in the organization have many perspectives. Therefore, if effort is made to make the vision "speak to" the special interests of all these groups, the vision could soon become meaningless. For this reason, it is a good rule of thumb that a statement of vision be no more than about one paragraph in length. Remember, there are two critical questions:

 ♦ What do we want this organization to become?

 ♦ What would "becoming" look like?

FIGURE 1.2 DIAGRAM OF CHANGE

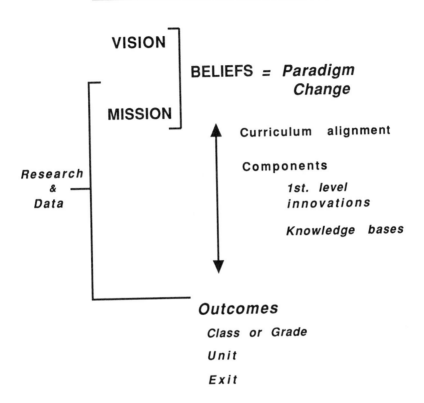

The second question (becoming) does not need to be stated as part of the vision, but it should be asked constantly as the vision of the organization is developed. Of course, it will be answered as the other components are assessed. An easy way to separate the vision and the mission of an organization is as follows:

A **Vision** is in reference to future direction—
A **Mission** is in reference to present purpose—

There is also some concern as to when the belief system is formulated and how this relates to the new paradigm. Most appropriately, the new paradigm is an interpreter of reality. It represents a way of viewing the institution in terms of the

vision, mission, and supporting belief system. (See APPENDIX—
ORANGE COUNTY PUBLIC SCHOOLS BELIEF SYSTEM, which was
developed in support of the vision, mission, and learning outcomes as a sample.)

If the select and sort-bell curve mentality is the paradigm
(view of reality), it is appropriate to believe that, perhaps,
25% of student grades shall be in the "F" and "D" categories
and that dropouts are natural. Under this belief system, teach,
test, and grade is an acceptable teaching model, and pop
quizzes are appropriate to make sure that students keep up
with homework. All of those procedures are perceived valid
in terms of that obsolete concept of reality.

Conversely, if a new paradigm is accepted whereby all
students are expected to be successful learners, it will be quite
natural to begin to challenge these practices as out of line
with the mission, and very few D's and F's will be expected.
Practices which "trip up" students such as pop quizzes will
soon be challenged. When professionals begin to recognize
that some practices are inconsistent with the mission and belief
system, this is a sign that change is beginning.

TIME GAINS SIGNIFICANCE—DIFFERENTLY

Factors which drive the old select and sort mission of
education come, in part, from the custodial nature of schools.
The school is expected to warehouse students who move along
at predetermined rates. *When* the students learn is important,
more important than *how completely* they learn.

Under the new mission, how completely students learn
becomes the focus. When they learn becomes subject to teaching
skills needed to bring about the complete learning. As a result
of this change, the passion for covering material gives way
to achieving outcomes. This concept was explained in *A Model
Of School Learning* by John Carroll who believed that learning
was a product of the time and instruction needed to learn
rather than simply the ability to learn (9).

Time becomes the tool of the school. When the mission
is changed, time is manipulated to complement purposes.
Changing time from a limiter to an enabler is one of the most
effective weapons in the arsenal to assure learning for all.

"Utilizing time" needs additional explanation. Usually in schools there is a set time limit to learn. In the secondary school, this is dictated by the Carnegie unit. In the elementary school, the broad spectrum of subjects which must be attended to limits time.

Suppose a student or a group of students need additional time to learn. Typically, it is not provided. The material is covered, the students are tested, grades are given, and the instructional process moves on. Those who have not yet learned the material must take lower grades and move on with incomplete learning. For the student who has learned incompletely, this process becomes a vicious cycle in which the student gets farther and farther behind.

The critical question is: How can time be provided to those who are not yet ready for the summative test? Some examples for extending time are volunteer aides, cooperative groups, special sessions before or after school for remedial learning (and also enrichment), special lunch groups, etc. With determination, other solutions can be generated. Computer technology offers some interesting possibilities. The Mastery Learning Model is certainly a model for providing time for complete learning (10).

Secondary schools are allowing additional time, even with the limitations of the Carnegie units, by block scheduling or providing service periods within the traditional six- or seven-period structure. Typically, the service period is a little shorter than other periods. It is scheduled at the beginning or end of the day or coupled with the lunch period.

Block scheduling is a concept which is being employed by secondary schools at an increasing rate. There appears to be considerable merit in block scheduling as a tool for breaking out of the time restraints of the old Carnegie unit. However, even where accreditation and state legal requirements make Carnegie units necessary, block scheduling can still work. There are several schemes. One of the less complicated plans is the four-period day with each period about 85 minutes long. A typical student schedule would include three periods for classes, and one period for research, study, or activities. A Carnegie unit is earned in each subject in one semester. This means the typical student would earn six or more units per year. (For additional information on the four-period day, see Edwards (11).)

Frazier and Sickles, in the *Directory of Innovations in High Schools*, list several innovative high school programs in which a common factor was getting control of time. Some type of block scheduling was used in many of the cited programs (12).

OUTCOMES

In a reform process, several levels of outcomes are needed, and once outcomes are identified, we work backwards through the curriculum to make sure that the necessary skills leading to their accomplishment are taught. Exit or general outcomes are first. They state the skills and knowledge students should have upon completing the system. Typical exit outcomes include statements such as:

♦ Students shall possess the basic skills necessary to succeed in a vocation or in higher education,

♦ Each student will become a self-directed learner.

The exit outcomes should be sufficiently comprehensive in order that a few outcomes identify the final expectancies. They are the accomplishments to be demonstrated by those who have been successful learners.

The exit outcomes will drive decisionmaking. They will become a part of the new paradigm—a reference point for productive efforts. Below, as an example, are the exit outcomes used in one school system. (Additional information is offered in Chapter 2.)

♦ EVERYONE WILL . . .

• Exhibit responsibility and self-discipline.

• Respect self, others, and environment.

• Use critical thinking, problem solving, and communication skills.

• Acquire a broad base of knowledge and experience.

• Be a self-directed learner.

Exit outcomes must be identified with the broadest level of input possible. (*A Special Note:* The use of the term "outcomes" may contribute to misunderstanding in some states or localities. It's important to adopt a new mission, identify what is wanted as the end product(s), and in the process utilize the results of research and data. This process does not require the use of the term, outcomes—or any other for that matter.)

It is defeating to adopt outcomes from an outside source. They must be developed in each school system and in each school. It is advisable for schools to convene committees and subcommittees which include parents, business leaders, political leaders, teachers, students, administrators, and support personnel.

Development of outcomes is an exercise in collaboration. The identification of outcomes is one of the most effective ways to get broad involvement in the change process.

A question may arise about the inclusion of business leaders and politicians in the process of setting outcomes since either group has the potential of directing outcomes toward a very narrow agenda. For example, the concept of educating the total individual might give way to a narrow agenda of producing workers, perhaps due to overemphasis upon the agenda of the Business Round Table in some state departments of education.

It must be recognized that the business and political sectors are significant partners of education. Broad input from partners is necessary, but the educator must maintain balance. Educators should support the concept of a competitive economy as one of the reasons for school reform, but this agenda must include developing responsible inventive citizens.

The individual school should ratify systemwide outcomes if they exist. It is appropriate for the individual school to add to the existing outcomes, but use the system outcomes as parameters. Of course, if the local school system has not yet embarked upon school reform, the individual school will need to work independently. Strong support from the central office is necessary. If the state has outcomes, then they also must guide local system.

Once exit outcomes are decided, they drive the development of the class or course outcomes and the unit outcomes. The establishment of outcomes leads quite naturally to the question, "What must be done to get what we want?" This is another point of entrance for research and data, and this is also the point of entrance for components.

It is a new experience for some educators to (a) know in clear and concise terms what they want, and (b) to be involved in the process of deciding what it will take to get what they want. Current practice must always be viewed in the light of research and data, and educators should consistently ask, "Will current practice get what we want?"

COMPONENTS

The very important innovations and practices which will help a reformed organization move forward are the components. They are the knowledge bases of data and research. They are procedures, techniques, and even different ways of doing business. As previously stated, components will not provide contextual change, but they will contribute mightily to making it have the need-fulfilling qualities necessary. Some additional examples of components are:

- ◆ Reality Therapy
- ◆ Instructional Models
- ◆ Cooperative Group Learning
- ◆ Scheduling Schemes
- ◆ Accountability Measures
- ◆ Research-Based Teaching Strategies
- ◆ Quality
- ◆ A Common Core of Learning

THE BACK DOOR

Components will not create level two change, but they may be used to create awareness of need or "loss of innocence." This happened in the author's own school system. For brevity, this is an oversimplification, but the following exemplifies the back door approach:

Reality therapy was adopted as a disciplinary philosophy and mastery learning was adopted as an instructional philosophy. Other than this, it was business as usual. Most other policies and procedures were leftover from the select and sort era. A review of grades, dropouts, and achievement demonstrated a bell-shaped curve mentality remained. As might be anticipated, very mixed success was experienced with mastery learning. This mixed success was due to an inconsistent belief system among the staff. It was finally recognized that a paradigm change was needed. A state of dissonance was created which backed us into embarking upon a long-term effort at changing the institutional reality of the organization.

HOW LONG DOES IT TAKE?

To make a contextual change which embraces the adoption of all factors listed in the model (Fig. 1.2) plus several research-based components will take 5 to 7 years. The average length of time required to get 75% or 85% of the staff to "own" the new paradigm is about 4 or 5 years. This estimation of time may seem excessive, but this is the consensus of several leaders who have initiated, "systemic" change (13).

The time required for such a change is a serious problem. There is a tendency to assume that an organization can be changed in 3 years, but 3 years will usually produce only surface change. To allow the depth required for the new reality to become a point of reference takes longer.

Time is a more serious problem in urban school systems because the leadership may not last long enough for change to reach the level of adoption required to survive the leader. In all school systems, state and local politics may get in the way of change. The time required for change statewide is even longer than at the local level. In the meantime, elections may change leadership and policymakers.

Recently, Larry W. Lezotte said (albeit tongue in cheek), "If I were President, I would work with Congress and declare a 3-year moratorium on firing superintendents and then turn them loose on reforming education." Of course, as just discussed, 3 years might not be long enough.

Lezotte also expressed concern that at some point specialization in this country caused superintendents to become managers: If reform is to happen, the superintendency must return to instructional leadership.

There may be only two ways to change an organization with a revolving door at the top:

♦ Put together a transition team composed of persons not usually subjected to the instability of the few top positions. The composition of this team must include school board members and influential political and business leaders.

♦ Employ a new leader who has worked with contextual change and who understands the new mission of education. A similar situation is true for school board members—elect those who support change or begin to train the new board members the week after election.

Organizational frustration, which often accompanies change, may focus upon a single issue and cause the loss of school board members. It is the responsibility of the reformers to recognize this potential and to mitigate it, if possible, through involvement and communication.

Some examples of activities and situations which have become the focal point of frustration resulting in leadership turnover are:

♦ Resistance to a new grading structure.

♦ Placing responsibility for the frustration on a single leader and electing board members who promise to remove him.

♦ Religious groups who fix upon some aspect of the reform as being sinful or threatening for some other reason.

♦ "Stakeholders" in the old structure who organize resistance due to being threatened.

♦ School board members who believe in the old select and sort paradigm and pass policies which send crippling messages from the top.

♦ Resistance to abandoning the bell curve (literally believing that "children must experience failure to learn to deal with the realities of life").

♦ Greed—The belief that to help all students succeed will dilute the benefits for upper middle class achievers.

There may be as many potential pitfalls as letters in the alphabet. Those listed above are just some which have actually been observed or encountered by the author. Let's reemphasize that *communication and education* are the keys to preventing resistance to change from becoming a focal issue.

If an issue such as one of those listed gathers steam before it is addressed, the task of management is difficult. It is important to begin immediately to *sell* the new paradigm, the vision, and the mission, and share a summary of additional work and actions needed to help keep momentum. This must be done with the planning and zeal of a *new bond issue*.

Considering the depth of effort needed, the tendency to protect the old paradigm, and the other inhibitors, it is understandable why reform is so difficult. Reform is not a choice, however—it is a necessity.

Finally, what might a restructured school look like which does not adhere to the bell curve paradigm? The following is offered as a starter:

♦ A passion for all students to become successful learners.

♦ A passion for quality—both physical and psychological.

♦ A productive climate.

♦ Identified outcomes for school—for the class or subject, and each unit.

♦ Continuous assessment, *i.e.*, asking questions such as "How is our school meeting its mission?" "Are all of our practices consistent with our belief system?" "How are my students doing?"

♦ Opportunities for children with different learning styles in academics and other activities.

♦ An insistence that all teachers be competent and

perform accordingly. This must be institutionalized and a part of the school culture.

+ Few or no grades of "C" or below. Grades below
"C" would represent incomplete learning. Incom-
pletes ("I's") are used until learning is more
complete, and students are expected to remove
the "I's."

+ An instructional organizational system which
provides for retesting and additional time for
students to bring learning to a state of completion, at least a "C" grade.

+ A constantly evolving way of managing and
of teaching which uses research and data to
achieve excellence.

+ An operational style which allows need-fulfill-
ment for teachers and students.

+ A disciplinary structure which is consistent with
the mission and belief system.

+ An alignment of the curriculum in all major
areas in order that parents, teachers, and administrators can understand where students have
been, where they are going, and who is responsible.

+ A belief system collaboratively prepared which
is based on a system of ethics.

These characteristics are by no means an attempt to provide
a prescription for the restructured and reformed school. In
fact, an important element of paradigm change is for all reformers to identify needs to accomplish the vision and subsequent
mission.

Some items listed as characterizing the restructured school
are subject to misunderstanding. For example, there are those
who contend that assessment of outcomes belongs with the
old model, "more management by objectives."

The author believes that comparing the creation of outcomes
with management by objectives is the result of misunderstanding
both. Due to a misapplication, both concepts are considered

the "bean-counter" kind of approach by some critics. Outcomes methods simply dictate an up-front decision about specific qualities that will indicate a fulfilled mission. Outcome-based education is a tool for celebrating complete learning.

SUMMARY

Finally, there is now hope for a new day for education in the United States. It has been more than a decade since *A Nation At Risk* sounded a national alarm about the need to reform education. Many misdirected efforts have come and gone, and the results have been marginal. Educators everywhere are beginning to recognize that trying to fix the old select and sort model will not suffice.

Lest there be misunderstanding, this is not a criticism of *A Nation At Risk*. This document had value: it possibly prevented the Department of Education from being disassembled, it fueled the drive for educational reform, and it indirectly produced "hindsight" wisdom that first order change would not produce needed results.

The solution to the school reform agenda is not to add additional innovations even though they may be worthwhile. A new paradigm must be developed. There must be a persistent determination to move beyond the bell curve. Every practice in the realm of public education must be called into question and a judgment must be made as to whether or not results fit the new paradigm or are throwbacks to the past.

There is significant dissatisfaction with public education in the United States. Public education is viewed incorrectly due to circumstances in 15 or 20 major cities across the country. Solving problems with education in the big cities will take a comprehensive approach, which includes strengthening family and child protection laws. The publicity emanating from these areas causes assumptions about education which are not true. As mentioned earlier, however, public education, even where it currently excels, is not adequate to meet the new demands of society.

More than 90% of the school systems enroll fewer than 10,000 students. Reform is important for these systems because the requirements for success are not as dependent upon extraneous factors. Reform may be somewhat easier in their more stable environments. Even though there is considerable variance in school systems in the United States and Canada, the need for reform and the tools for reform are similar. All districts need to respond to the new mission which has emerged. A significant problem is failure of reformers to recognize the depth of changed required.

Change has been described in this chapter as composed of two levels, tinkering and contextual change. Level one involves all the actions taken which are designed to improve the existing model of schooling. Level two changes are those designed to create a new model.

Paradigm, as used here, means a view of reality. All aspects of education are viewed in accordance with and in reference to a paradigm. The old paradigm views reality for education in terms of the select and sort-bell curve model. A new paradigm should view education in terms of success for all students.

Educational reform requires a new vision, a new mission, and a belief system which complements both. All this must drive the new paradigm. This leads to second level change, in which first level components become valuable resources.

Reform is slow, and will require several years of hard work. In the meantime, involvement and sharing with "stakeholders" takes on new importance.

Political realities require that standardized assessment must be addressed because of political realities, but reformers need to avoid letting standardized tests indict reform efforts. Attend to standardized tests, and then get back to other assessments which accomplish the mission.

Finally, in a reform effort, communication, education, and involvement are the essential elements for sustaining progress

REFERENCES

1. Glenn E. Robinson, *Learning Expectancy, A Force Changing Education* (Feb. 1986). Educational Research Service, Arlington, VA 22209.

2. William Glasser, M.D., *QUALITY SCHOOL: Managing Students Without Coercion* (1990). Harper & Row, Publishers, Inc.,

10 East 53rd Street, New York, NY 10022.

3. Joe Schneider and Paul Hudson, *Exploding The Myths: Another Round In The Education Debate*. American Association of School Administrators, 1801 North Moore Street, Arlington, VA 22209, pg. 3.

4. David T. Kearns and Denis P. Doyle, *Winning The Brain Race: A Bold Plan To Make Our Schools Competitive* (1989). ICS Press, Institute for Contemporary Studies, 243 Kearny Street, San Francisco, CA 94108, pg. 133.

5. John Hiliary, *Paradigm Change: More Magic Than Logic* (1990). OUTCOMES–9, 1925 W. County Road, Box 2, Roseville, MN 55113–2791.

6. *Ibid.*

7. Lonnie Harp, "Reform Law Meets Rear-Guard Reaction in Eastern Kentucky" (Dec. 9, 1993). *Education Week*, Vol. XII, No. 14., pg. 1.

8. Daniel V. Levine and Allan C. Ornstein, "Reforms That Can Work—These Tested-and-True Approaches Show Promise for Improving the Performance of Low Achievers" (June 1993). *The American School Board Journal*, pg. 33.

9. John A. Carroll, "A Model Of School Learning" (1963). *Teachers College Record*, pp. 64, 723–733.

10. Thomas R. Guskey, *Implementing Mastery Learning* (1985). Wadsworth Publishing Company, Belmont, CA 94002.

11. Clarence M. Edwards, Jr., "The Four-Period Day: Restructuring to Improve Student Performance" (May 1993). *NAASP Bulletin*, Vol. 77, No. 553.

12. Gloria G. Frazier and Robert Sickles, *The Directory of Innovations In High Schools* (use Index under "Schedule," "Block") (1993). Eye On Education, Box 388, Princeton Junction, NJ 08550.

13. L.W. Lezotte and B.A. Bancroft, "Growing Use of Effective School Model for School Improvement" (1985). *Educational Leadership*, pgs. 23–27, 42.

2

NEW WAYS OF DOING BUSINESS

INTRODUCTION

In the previous chapter, "components" were identified as those changes in education which, within themselves, will not change education significantly. It was noted, however, that as part of a mission change and a new paradigm for education, components and innovations become extremely valuable.

The idea that all students are to become successful learners means exactly that—all! To obscure the concept with reference to ability, aptitude, socioeconomic background, or for any other of a host of delimiters is not acceptable. Again, the expectancy must be that *all* students will learn. This stress on *all* is at the very heart of the effort to move beyond the bell curve because the bell curve represents a model in which about one-half of the students do not learn very well (1).

Conditions which led to the new mission and the resulting expectancies for change in education are:

♦ Society can no longer afford large numbers of basically unemployable marginally educated workers.

♦ Business and industry cannot compete in the international market unless employees have skills that exceed current levels.

♦ It is recognized that all children can learn. Whether or not they do is a matter of time and teaching skill, not student ability.

Figure 2.1 rewords the new mission and related factors. There are many ways to state the new mission, but always included is success or learning for all students. To state it simply, a contextual change is represented by a mission statement such as the one in Figure 2.1, but it will be institutionalized only if each component in the school is evaluated for consistency or alignment. Remember, almost every aspect of current schooling reflects the paradigm of the old model.

This chapter discusses a few activities useful for reforming an educational program. Factors needing alignment, outlined in Figure 2.1, also are discussed. A goal is to demonstrate how some promising, research-based practices can be incorporated into an effort to move beyond the bell curve.

FIGURE 2.1 THE NEW MISSION OF EDUCATION

MISSION

All Students Will Be Successful LEARNERS—

Components to assess

- Grouping Patterns
- Grading Practices
- Research-Based Teaching Practices
- Parental Involvement
- Empowering Teachers
- Teacher Evaluation
- Outcomes

ACHIEVING THE NEW MISSION

If the new mission for the successful school is to be realized, the factors listed in Figure 2.1 must be carefully evaluated to be certain that each strengthens and supports the mission.

At present, these practices are used to support the old mission. Perhaps, this is because it is not broadly recognized that restructuring means mission alignment. Once a mission which is different from the select and sort bell-shaped tradition is recognized, a new way of using selected factors is possible.

The factors listed comprise some of the main areas which merit the careful attention of school reformers. There are other key areas, such as school climate and student activities, which merit entire chapters of their own. In an effort to clarify some of the changes which must be made in aligning the school with the new mission, some of the factors listed in Figure 2.1 are discussed in the pages which follow—others need an entire chapter.

GROUPING PATTERNS

There is now a considerable body of research which supports heterogeneous grouping for almost all students. The only possible exceptions are for those who pose a danger for others and those in certain advanced classes designed for a specific purpose at the high school level.

Homogeneous grouping practices emerged at a time when most children were not expected to learn very much. This practice has potential to harm a sizable number of students, and is nothing more than an educational promulgation of intellectual and social inequities.

This condemnation of homogeneous grouping applies equally to special education. When children are placed in separate "ability" groups, stigmas can develop and expectancies change, and the outcome is usually undesirable.

It will be easier to change grouping practices for nonhandicapped students than for handicapped students, however. This, of course, is due to the host of state and federal laws designed to protect the handicapped, but, sadly, the same laws hamper innovation. The laws have helped create a constituency supported by a cartel of lawyers and professional advocates, all with a very narrow focus, fueled by a measure of self-interest. To consider another model threatens the status quo with its legalistic base. In reality, homogeneous grouping results in students being labeled and having imposed upon them limitations which, in fact, are not valid.

In special education, efforts at heterogenous grouping are sometimes known as the process of inclusion. Inclusion is an idea whose time has come for the following reasons:

+ Special education has become a dumping ground for children who are different, all under the banner of "appropriate placement."

+ Once identified for special education, a student tends to remain there.

+ Student learning is reduced greatly in special education.

+ Special education has become stifled by regulation and red tape.

College teachers have been known to tell regular teacher candidates to avoid recruiters representing school systems which use the inclusion model. This is due to two causes: (a) Inclusion is viewed as a technique to avoid special education requirements and cost, and (b) regular teachers are expected to meet the needs of special education students without the necessary support and training. However, early opposition to inclusion has subsided with the apparent success of some models.

Inclusion must not be viewed as a means to escape the special education yoke. The term yoke is used only with reference to regulation, the endless paperwork and meetings required. If done correctly, it is a plan for breaking the homogeneous prison of special education students. The resources which are devoted to special students must follow them into the regular placement and take the form of training and support for the regular teacher and assistance for the special student.

The inclusion model may eventually impact upon the tendency to refer almost every child that is different for a special education eligibility assessment. If every student is expected to be a successful learner, and if the inclusion model carries appropriate resources, referrals should decrease.

Parents of special students may be reluctant to accept heterogeneous grouping as the most productive practice. The special education cartel is not the only group that may resist heterogeneous grouping. Heavy resistance often comes from the parents of the brightest children, who may perceive any change as experimentation and think their children will be held back.

The fact is, all children benefit from the heterogeneous classroom. This statement may be challenged by those who continue to believe that tracking manages student diversity successfully. Ironically, tracking and homogeneous grouping persist in the face of overwhelming evidence that they are ineffective generally and harmful in consequence for many students.

Paul George made several suggestions as to the cause for this persistence of tracking. One of his hypotheses is that the political realities of education may intervene:

> ". . . [I]t is possible that tracking persists so tenaciously, in spite of the results for the great majority of the students, partially because of the parents of a small group of students who sometimes appear to benefit. Parents of the top ten percent of students in American public schools tend to be sophisticated in their understanding of the politics of school district decision-making and skillful in their ability to influence those decisions.
>
> ". . . [W]ho can blame educators from paying attention to what these parents say, especially when their sentiments are reinforced for years from the highest levels of the state and Federal governments?" (2)

Jeannie Oakes offers reasons related to the context of schooling:

> " . . . [A]n analysis of these schooling and societal contexts suggests that teaching profoundly influences the day-to-day conduct of secondary schools and both reflects and interacts with fundamental assumptions about how schools should respond to student diversity. This contextual view of tracking permits a fuller understanding of why teaching is not easily reconsidered or changed" (3).

The concepts of both George and Oakes about the political

and societal context of tracking and homogeneous grouping leads to identifying this practice as a reflection of the select and sort role which society expected of the schools. A consistent strand running throughout this book is that of the need to rethink traditional practices, making decisions on the basis of research and data while looking at every practice of the school which is a reflection of the old mission.

Good and Brophy also explained some of the most undesirable effects of ability grouping, even in-class grouping, as follows:

"... First, ability grouping tends to exaggerate preexisting differences in achievement rates by accelerating the progress of students in the top groups but slowing the progress of students in the bottom groups (Rowan & Miracle, 1983; Weinstein, 1976). This effect is especially pronounced when the groups are truly homogeneous and notably different from one another (Hallinan & Sorensen, 1983) and when the teacher emphasizes the distinctions between groups and treats the groups notably differently (Gamoran, 1984). Second, high groups seem to benefit not only from faster pacing but from a higher quality of instruction from the teacher (Cazden, 1985; Hiebert, 1983) and from a more desirable work orientation and higher level of attention to the lesson (Eder & Felmlee, 1984). Third, although in theory grouping should be done to meet students' individual needs and should be marked by frequent regrouping and movement of individual students between groups, in practice group membership tends to remain highly stable once groups are formed initially (Hallinan & Sorensen, 1983). Furthermore, since students spend more time with peers in their groups than they do with classmates assigned to other groups, group assignments affect peer contact and friendship patterns in addition to achievement rates, the more so as time goes on (Hallinan & Sorensen, 1985). In mixed-race classrooms where race is correlated with reading ability or achievement levels, ability grouping will result in de facto resegregation of the students, even though race as such may not be taken into account in making group assignments (Haller, 1985). Finally, ability grouping can result in the labeling effects, 'low- group psychology' effect, and related undesirable expectation effects that were reviewed in Chapter 4" (4).

The author has a personal friend who is well-educated, but not an educator. Much to the shock of a mutual group of friends, this person pulled his child out of the public elementary school. When asked why he had done such a thing, his reply was, "If one is sentenced for a crime he eventually gets out of jail. If my child remained in his placement in the low group, his sentence is forever, and he will have weak teachers, poor models, low expectancies, and his prognosis for ever achieving in school will be exceedingly poor." I had no retort, for I knew my noneducator friend was correct. In fact, the administrative staff had met only a week earlier to lay plans to abandon the homogeneous structure. Can such an arrangement of students in homogeneous groups be justified in light of the research which is available?

The discussion above is not intended to present an in-depth analysis of ability grouping. The author believes that this issue has been settled in the research for about a decade. However, knowing is not enough! In some communities, to change grouping practices requires diplomacy. A headlong move into a new practice may be a dangerous move. Like all changes, this one must begin with communication. (*Note:* Additional information on and an excellent analysis of homogeneous grouping is available from the Educational Research Service, 2000 Clarendon Boulevard, Arlington, VA 22201. Another excellent resource is, *How To Untrack Your School*, by Paul George (5).)

Some communities operate the public elementary school like an elite private school for a small part of the student population. Certain students of socially astute parents are placed in the "high" group. This group has the nice parties, the finest instructional material, wonderful field trips, and visiting artists. The local social structure dictates the children selected for this class. "Of course, it's better for children to be with their own friends!," is a familiar statement.

An interesting case involved the schools in Richmond, Virginia. This is a city of predominately minority students, with a minority superintendent and school board. A practice of clustering certain white students in at least two elementary schools was revealed. Of course, it immediately became a subject of controversy. If the expectancy is learning for all students, if quality is expected, and time is the controlled variable, such arrangements should not be attractive or necessary.

Teachers may initially oppose heterogeneous grouping because they don't know how to meet the needs of a diverse group of children. There are several ways to help the teacher work effectively with a heterogeneous group. All of the following steps have been utilized effectively by some schools:

- Reducing the pupil-teacher ratio. This does not necessarily mean employing additional teachers (use teams, aides, volunteers, and scheduling schemes).

- Recruiting parent and senior citizen volunteers.

- Providing inservice assistance for teachers about how to structure the lessons in a way to provide extra time for students who take longer to learn and enrichment for those who learn quickly.

- Creating cooperative groups.

- Providing teachers time to set up enrichment centers for students who learn quickly and remedial exercises for those who learn at a slower pace.

- Regrouping students for reading and, perhaps, math.

The last item may be misleading. This is not a disguised reversion to homogeneous grouping. It is, however, recommended if other conditions, i.e., political pressure or policy, require that some homogeneous grouping be retained. Good and Brophy (6) provide a suggestion for regrouping which accommodates needs to limit diversity while maintaining the benefits of the heterogeneous group. Any special purpose grouping such as reading groups should be clearly ungrouped for other parts of the curriculum. The goal is to avoid a low group with low expectations and low self-esteem. If this can't be accomplished completely, the plan as outlined by Good and Brophy will help, at least, for part of the day.

One can kill the effectiveness of heterogeneous grouping by not providing teachers support through staff development and supervision. Teaching a class with diverse levels of learning requires skill, and it is the responsibility of administrators to provide necessary assistance. Untrained teachers may react by teaching to the mean while neglecting the quick learners and the slow learners. This is the fear of the parents of "high achievers," and if this happens, the result will be pressure from parents to return to homogeneous grouping.

Possibly the first action for at risk learners is to provide them with positive role models, such as bright achievers. For gifted students, there are numerous opportunities to excel in a heterogeneous classroom. There appears to be very little, if any, benefit in separating gifted students except, perhaps, in secondary school.

Finally, a word about an inappropriate practice of homogeneous grouping: many states have created residential schools for the gifted. This is nothing more than an elitist form of homogeneous grouping. This practice needs careful study. What happens when a student is taken from a leadership role in his or her home school, for example? What replaces the opportunity for most gifted students to learn leadership in school activities? What happens to a class in the home school when several leaders and role models are removed? There are benefits for the gifted student in a regular high school. They learn skills in a mini-society which has elements of the larger society, and they can learn to appreciate their own uniqueness as they adjust to a diversity of peers. There is one other factor—in a large number of secondary schools, the college prep program offers several advanced placement courses and even college courses. Gifted students from such programs compete quite well in college with those who have attended special schools.

Heterogeneous grouping is a classroom structure which

can support most effectively the concept of learning for all. It helps in efforts to abandon the bell curve. This practice is supported by research as being the most productive way of organizing students.

GRADING

One of the primary tasks for those who wish to lead in school reform is to assess the grading practices within the school (7). The school principal should share the following expectancies with teachers relative to grading:

◆ The bell-shaped curve is not an appropriate device for assigning grades. Instruction is *intervention*, and it will not cause a group of students to rank according to the normal curve of distribution (bell curve). With appropriate instruction, the curve should always be positively skewed.

◆ A large number of A and B grades does not indicate soft standards, but is more likely to be a sign of successful instruction. Of course, as mentioned, standards and expectancies must remain high.

◆ A large number of low grades is one indication that the teacher may have failed to teach the skills needed or to provide enough time for some students to learn.

◆ Grading practices should encourage students, not discourage them.

How a teacher averages grades can adversely affect the students. For example, if summative and formative grades are mixed or zeros are given and added to the student's grade average, then the student will receive inappropriately low grades.

The need to separate summative and formative tests has been an aspect of grading that many teachers have not understood. Summative grades are those which should count in assigning grades for the report card. They are either the result of unit tests or the teacher's best judgment of what the student has accomplished (in summary). Formative grades are the result of checking homework and of using sampling techniques such as quizzes to check for understanding. They tell the teacher whether additional instruction is needed.

A problem with grading usually occurs when the teacher does not differentiate between summative and formative activities and combines them for the final grade. This usually results in the student receiving grades which are based upon incomplete instruction. In reality, the summative grade should be assigned only after a formative check has revealed the areas needing a reteach, and after the student has been taught any missing skills.

Grades must never be used as a tool of discipline. The following practices have been observed: (a) points taken off for disciplinary infractions, (b) negative grades added to the grade record for not doing homework or an assignment, such as a zero for the day, (c) pop quizzes given as punishment for inattentive behavior, and (d) points cut for lateness or other infractions. These and other similar practices result in grades which do not reflect what the child actually knows.

The zero is a savage grade! Zeros should never be given. If grades reflect learning, then the zero indicates that nothing was learned. If a student simply sits in class, something is learned. In fact, something is learned even if the student is not in class. A zero deludes and diminishes to such an extent that a student can't overcome its effect. No score below 50 or 60 should be included in a grade average. In fact, it's best to give an incomplete and use retesting.

Retesting causes extra work for the teachers. This is the reason for using formative assessments—to reduce the number of students needing a retest. Another teacher concern is that students will rely on the retest and not study the first time around. This will not happen if students have to qualify for the retest by doing extra preparation to assure that they are ready for the retest. An example was cited by a parent in a recent conversation. His son was enrolled in a calculus class where the teacher had a retest policy. One night, the student was studying late. The concerned parent said, "Please go to bed, you can take a retest if you don't do well." The reply was, "I don't want to do the extra work to qualify for a retest —I want to do well the first time."

Installing a policy for the retest is a way to make summative grades more productive for the students (see Fig. 2.2).

USE OF RESEARCH IN TEACHING

During the last 10 or 15 years, educators have learned more about what works in teaching than in the previous 50 years. Teaching is now a full-blown profession with the unique knowledge base which a profession requires. Accordingly, decisions relative to instruction and teaching should be based upon research or data.

It is essential that all involved in school reform become informed about recent knowledge in education. This only can be done through independent study or by enrolling in formal classes. The following are suggested as a starting point for those who wish to increase their knowledge about effective practices:

Reality Therapy—

> William Glasser, *Control Theory; A New Explanation Of How We Control Our Lives* (1984), Harper and Row, 10 East 53rd St., New York, NY 10022.

> William Glasser, *The Quality School, Managing Students Without Coercion* (1990), Harper and Row, 10 East 53rd St., New York, NY 10022.

Cooperative Learning—

> Ruth Parker, "Small Group Cooperative Learning In The Classroom" (March 1984), *OSSC Bulletin*, 1787 Agate Street, University of Oregon, Eugene, OR, 97403.

> David W. Johnson, et. al., *Circles Of Learning: Cooperation In The Classroom* (1988), ASCD, 125 N. Pitt Street, Alexandria, VA 22314.

Outcome-Based Education—

> Contact The Network For Outcome Based Schools, Johnson City Schools, 666 Reynolds Road, Johnson City, NY 13790.

FIGURE 2.2 RETEST?—WHY NOT??

A VERY EFFECTIVE WAY TO MAKE GRADING PRACTICES ENCOURAGING FOR STUDENTS IS WITH THE RETEST

HERE'S HOW!

- ANY STUDENT WHO WISHES MAY TAKE A RETEST.
- A RETEST IS ANOTHER FORM OF THE TEST FOR THE SAME SKILLS.
- A RETEST IS NOT A GIFT, IT IS AN EARNED OPPORTUNITY.
- A RETEST CAN ONLY BE EARNED IF A STUDENT DOES THE EXTRA WORK TO PROVE THAT HE OR SHE IS READY.
- A RETEST CAN ONLY BE TAKEN WITHIN CERTAIN TIME LIMITS (*e.g.*, 10 DAYS).
- THE GRADE OF THE RETEST MAY REPLACE THAT OF THE OLD TEST BUT A RETEST CANNOT LOWER THE GRADE.

HERE'S WHY . . .

- ALL STUDENTS HAVE OCCURRENCES IN THEIR LIVES WHICH CAUSE DISTRACTION AND, PERHAPS, A LOWER GRADE.
- THIS IS AN EXCELLENT WAY FOR A TEACHER TO GET THE STUDENT TO TAKE RESPONSIBILITY FOR EXTRA WORK.
- REGARDLESS OF HOW TALENTED THE TEACHER, OCCASIONALLY THERE WILL BE A MISCALCULATION AS TO THE STUDENTS' READINESS FOR THE SUMMATIVE TEST.
- STUDENTS WILL HAVE THE OPPORTUNITY TO MAKE HIGHER GRADES AND TO ACHIEVE AT A HIGHER LEVEL.

Mastery Learning—

Thomas R. Guskey, *Implementing Mastery Learning* (1985), Wadsworth Publishing Company, Belmont, CA 94002.

James H. Brock, H.C. Efthim, and Robert B. Burns, *Building Effective Mastery Learning Schools* (1989), Longman, Inc., 95 Church Street, White Plains, NY 10601.

Teaching Practices—

Thomas L. Good and Jere E. Brophy, *Looking In Classrooms* (4th ed., 1987), Harper and Row, 10 East 53rd Street, New York, NY 10022.

Joan L. Herman, Pamela R. Aschbacher, and Lynn Winters, *A Practical Guide To Alternative Assessment* (1992), Association for Supervision and Curriculum Development, 1250 N. Pitt Street, Alexandria, VA 22314.

Vito Perrone, *Expanding Student Assessment* (1991), Association for Supervision and Curriculum Development, 1250 N. Pitt Street, Alexandria, VA 22314.

Of course, this is not an exhaustive list. It is only a starting point. These resources can lead to an understanding of some of the primary assumptions which support the new mission of education. There are many other resources available about these topics.

Smith and Andrews (8), in a study of successful schools, found that a positive staff perception of the principal was enhanced by a belief that the principal was well-informed. The need for scholarship is essential for all who wish to go beyond the bell curve. Those in key roles as school reformers must understand the various knowledge bases that assist in efforts to make school a place for all children to learn.

Educators must devote the necessary time for study and professional reading is a must. Often administrators and teachers who grow professionally adopt professional reading as a hobby. A constant responsibility of the educator is to determine if each school practice, custom, or action is consistent with research. An effective measuring tool used by those involved in outcome-based education is the problem-solving procedure outlined in Figure 2.3.

When a faculty or a study group utilizes this process, the value of using research is highlighted and resistance to decisions is reduced. It is difficult to be a "hold out" when it is demonstrated by research that, "What we are doing will not get us what we want," or "What we are doing is not supported by research or data."

FIGURE 2.3 PROBLEM-SOLVING PROCEDURE

GROUP DECISION-MAKING PROCEDURE

♦ WHAT DO WE WANT?
  ♦ WHAT DOES RESEARCH SAY?
    ♦ WHAT ARE WE DOING?
      ♦ WHAT WILL GET US WHAT WE WANT?

PARENTAL INVOLVEMENT

There is often reluctance on the part of educators to involve parents as real partners in the school enterprise. Some of the following are frequently cited:

♦ They are not professional.
♦ Confidentiality is lost.
♦ They are not dependable.
♦ They tend to take over.

In the following discussion, ways to work with parents and possibly avoid some of the pitfalls will be explored. Primary ways to involve parents are serving as volunteers, members of project committees, members of advisory groups, as reinforcers, and as learners.

VOLUNTEERS

Most schools will never have the resources or personnel to meet the overwhelming needs of pupils who attend the typical elementary or secondary school. Success for all students means cutting through time limitations and shortages of resources in order to get the job done. Probably the greatest external resource available for expanding time to the school is the volunteer.

School volunteers come from three groups—parents, committed citizens (seniors or other committed workers), and older students. The parents are the most active. Teachers who have had no experience in working with volunteers need training prior to participating in a volunteer program. Extending time for a student usually means added time on task, such as working one-on-one. However, if the teacher doesn't know how to utilize the volunteer, this just provides one more person for whom to plan.

PROJECT COMMITTEES

Perhaps, one of the most useful tools in using project committees is the "unitary project." "Unitary Project" means a project with a beginning and a predefined end. This kind of project is very effective for both teachers and volunteers who are new to the process. Unitary projects are usually short, they have a single focus (a defined task), and the committee dissolves when the project is completed.

Many of the potential problems with volunteers are automatically resolved when the project is unitary and the plan for dissolving is made in advance. Some typical unitary projects might include:

+ Planning a holiday celebration.
+ Organizing a tutoring program.
+ Developing materials to supplement a reading program.
+ Working in concert with teachers to study a specific concern.

Involvement will give the parents ownership in the school.

There is an important secondary value in project committees and other types of parental involvement. Those in the school can get to know key community leaders, and when inevitable rumors and other problems surface, a base of communication is already established.

As previously mentioned, teachers who are to work with committees and other volunteers need some initial training. The principal, with the assistance of experienced teachers, can cover important points for those unexperienced in working with volunteers. Some important considerations in working with volunteers are:

+ *Confidentiality*—What are the teacher's responsibilities? What are the parents' responsibilities? How might "responsibilities" be approached with parents?

+ *Expectations*—When and how often will parents participate? Exactly what will the volunteer do? How will he or she be prepared?

+ *Assessment*—How can the volunteer be involved in assessment of the activity? Decide up front, "how we assess."

+ *Payment*—How will the volunteer be paid? "Volunteer" implies free; however, some payment is helpful as reinforcement. This should be planned.

+ *Alternatives*—What if the volunteer does not come when planned? This possibility must be considered, and alternatives should be available so time isn't lost.

REINFORCERS

Parents and other volunteers can be extremely positive promoters of the school. When they have ownership of the school due to their involvement, enthusiasm is enhanced. This enthusiasm is contagious. Parental enthusiasm affects the morale of the teachers, and it helps teachers to realize the importance of their contribution.

Parents become enthusiastic supporters of the school when they are invited to attend special activities, plan activities, take walking visits of the school, and view their children featured in programs and publications.

One successful principal invited 10 to 12 parents into the

school each week for coffee. Following a brief visit and a short talk about the school, the principal took the parents on a walking tour. He always had a short positive comment about the teachers they saw in action. The parents would invariably "leak" this information back to the teachers. At times, a "second hand" compliment has a special impact.

ADVISORY GROUPS

Those who practice asking parents, "How is the school doing?," use an effective and positive tool to receive information. Otherwise, they may learn this information in ways that are not so positive. The primary way to involve parents in assessment is through advisory groups. Parents may also be involved in assessment by helping to evaluate projects in which they are involved or through periodic surveys.

Assessment should always be the ending activity of the unitary project. In the military, a similar activity is known as "debriefing." The debriefing of parent volunteers at the end of a project is somewhat different, but similar as information is gathered. Of importance are such questions as:

♦ Did we accomplish our goals?

♦ What could we have done differently?

♦ Are there additional needs identified as a result of this project?

♦ What do we need to celebrate?

The need to celebrate cannot be mentioned without some clarification. There is so much to celebrate when committed persons work for students. Additionally, there is usually a real feeling of accomplishment when volunteers and professionals jointly complete a project. Why not capitalize upon this and make the "pat-on-the-back" an operational procedure?

PARENT SEMINARS

An increasing role of the school is to provide services for the parent. In fact, in some districts groups try to incorporate the school into a comprehensive family service unit which provides a full range of services such as child care, healthcare, parental training, nutrition, social services, and child protective services.

This approach has much appeal because learning is extremely difficult if some of these services are nonexistent. However, because of myriad regulations and "turf" problems, a comprehensive approach may be seen only in scattered pilot projects for the next few years.

Coordinating seminars through the school for parents is a way to connect the home and the school, as well as provide subject content to parents. Some of the subjects for parent seminars might be:

- ♦ Child nutrition
- ♦ Helping the child in school
- ♦ An introduction to instructional techniques such as cooperative learning, mastery teaching, and others,
- ♦ Special "how to" seminars in which parents learn various special skills, and
- ♦ Single parent seminars.

Seminars are usually most effective when they are of short duration. Three to six sessions are most successful, although longer ones may work if the parents have a particular interest in the topic and the instructor is talented.

All the things mentioned which involve parents— projects, committees, advisory groups, and seminars—are designed to share with parents a sense of ownership in the school. Of course, parents should be involved in the restructuring process from top to bottom, *i.e.,* defining mission, setting outcomes, and creating a vision. Remember, those who have ownership feel they have some control, and the feeling of control is the most important ingredient of empowerment.

EMPOWERING TEACHERS

The process of empowering teachers has much to do with ownership. Simply put, those who own an enterprise have a considerable stake in its success. Also, as previously stated, the principle byproduct of ownership is control. The human species has spent millions of years in an effort to control things in the environment. This inclination toward control is one of the strongest motivators.

It is assumed, and rightly so, if teachers have ownership, they will feel control; and if teachers have a feeling of control, two things will happen:

+ They will be productive and optimistic. They will want to make *positive* changes in the organization.

+ They can be brought into the decisionmaking process as partners, and their front-line expertise may be applied to improving the school.

Those on restructuring committees, school boards, and in central offices can exert some influence toward teacher empowerment, but the school principal is the critical person. Empowerment can become a vehicle through which the principal appropriately shares leadership. In the process of empowering teachers, the principal may have to give up some "traditionalship," but not the principalship (9).

The question arises as to how the principal can empower teachers without abdicating responsibility or letting the organization drift into chaos or anarchy. The following essential components are useful in a movement toward an empowering method of leadership:

+ The principal maintains primary control over the areas which are the basis of his or her personal accountability.

+ The principal works with subgroups of teachers to define empowerment.

+ The principal assists the staff in developing a mission statement.

+ The principal and staff develop a problemsolving model.

Each component is discussed briefly.

CONTROLLING BASICS OF PERSONAL ACCOUNTABILITY

Certain expectations must be insisted upon by the school principal regardless of how much empowerment teachers experience. These expectations involve operational management and ethical aspects of school leadership.

The principal must maintain control of the basic management of the school. Limitation of time and the learning needs of children simply will not allow committee management. Committee input is important, but final responsibility must be that of the principal. These management expectancies include:

♦ Building (physical plant) and Financial Management

♦ Policy and Work Rules Administration

♦ Ethical Responsibility

♦ Coordination

Of course, there are other responsibilities of the principal such as facilitating growth of the professional staff, accounting for outcomes, maintaining school climate, and showing instructional leadership. However, most of these functions can be accomplished very effectively and efficiently by utilizing the skills and expertise of the teaching staff. In many instances, an empowering principal becomes a facilitator.

Teacher empowerment must affect the professional aspects of the school which mold the daily life of the teachers. This includes such things as instructional methodology, developing new programs, creating innovative schedules, working on commonly identified problems, making personal recommendations, choosing materials, etc.

DEFINING EMPOWERMENT

There are those who see teacher empowerment as group management of the school. In fact, there have been a few experiments where the school has operated without a principal. Various responsibilities traditionally assigned to the principal were delegated to teachers. Reports from these experiments were not very encouraging. Generally, the morale of the teachers declined under the overwhelming press of responsibilities requiring time and emotional involvement which detracted from the primary goal of teaching.

Teacher empowerment is often cited when the need to

restructure schools is discussed. However, as mentioned earlier, teacher empowerment is just one element among the many components of the total school which must be affected. A new mission of learning for all students must become the basis for reevaluating every aspect of the school.

Again, teacher empowerment is simply involving teachers in the decisionmaking that concerns aspects of their professional work. It is characterized by open communication and team work between the principal and teachers. It does not take power away from the principal. Power has an unusual property. It does not diminish with sharing, but expands and becomes more effective.

To assure that the entire staff understands the meaning of empowerment, the principal should form a subcommittee of teachers to discuss the job responsibilities of the principal and of the teachers. This discussion should culminate in establishing empowerment procedures. A final result of this committee work should be a definitive report to the entire faculty. Some helpful focus points for this committee are:

♦ Teachers should be involved in interviewing and recommending new employees with whom they will work.

♦ Teachers should be involved in deciding a change in curriculum or in a decision about how to compensate for a diagnosed weakness.

♦ Teachers should select books and materials which will complement the program.

♦ Teachers should have the responsibility for staff development and formative assessment of colleagues.

♦ Teachers should have input in setting the calendar for the school year.

♦ Teachers should assist the principal in planning the year's budget.

♦ Teachers to be involved in setting the daily schedule of the school (within parameters which set minimum hours and amount of time on task).

Of course, there are countless other ways to involve teachers in an empowering school operation. If a principal or a school improvement committee can subscribe to at least five of the seven above points with a positive response, then, perhaps, this is indicative of a style of openness and receptivity needed.

Creating a core group and several subgroups is a vehicle for the principal to use in a teacher empowerment model. The core group of six or eight teachers should work with the principal in making many of the decisions typically handed down by the principal. The subgroups are used to study and report on specific problems or concerns. One or two subgroups might remain together for the entire school year, such as a staff development group and professional relations group, which make recommendations relative to team building. Other subgroups dissolve as tasks are completed.

The core group and, perhaps, several subgroups will work with the principal on the tasks yet to be discussed in this chapter. They are: learning to use a problemsolving model, devising a mission statement, and the critical task of setting outcomes. All of these activities will be productive only to the extent that teachers are involved. As part of a district's effort to restructure, the same tasks must be accomplished on a systemwide basis—both centrally and in each school.

USING A PROBLEM-SOLVING MODEL

A problem-solving model was outlined in Figure 2.3. It is called "a group decision-making procedure." This or some other procedure should be adopted. There is one additional question to add to Figure 2.3, and that is, *"Is the anticipated result consistent with our mission?"*

Some of the recommendations and procedures outlined in this discussion of teacher empowerment could change the basic style of operating the school. When teachers are involved in the effort to make schools better by identifying problem areas and planning improvement, real change can occur. Actually, this is "restructuring" without the vague and inappropriate statements which usually indict education.

THE DEVELOPMENT OF A MISSION STATEMENT

One of the most important activities for a staff is the development of a mission statement. This was discussed when considering teacher empowerment, but it is now appropriate to revisit. Actually, the mission relates to every other activity in the school. The school's mission is mentioned in several places in this book and has been a primary subject thus far. The fact is, unless the mission is known most work is similar to aimless wandering.

When the principal, staff, and parents engage in setting a mission, several factors must be considered:

♦ Does the school system have a mission, and how might the local school set a mission consistent with that of the system?

♦ What research should the staff explore prior to actually working on the mission?

Once the parameters of the school are decided, the staff must become informed about the new expectancies which society has for the schools as discussed in Chapter 1 and in other pertinent literature. The network of outcome-based education publishes a publication, *Outcomes*, which is an excellent source (see the address listed under knowledge bases earlier in this chapter).

Invariably, working on a mission statement will lead to a discussion of what is meant by "all children learning." Resolving just how much the staff can support the concept of *"all"* will require some very valuable group discussions and research. As the concept of *"all"* is explored, the bell curve and its limiting ramifications is likely to emerge. Setting a mission may very well be the first and most significant way of involving teachers. It is extremely empowering when the school's mission statement belongs to the staff.

OUTCOMES

Working with the staff to list student outcomes desired is the very next step after deciding a mission. Identifying desired outcomes is significant because outcomes bring the mission to fulfillment. Refer to Figure 2.4 relative to the relationship between the mission and outcomes.

FIGURE 2.4 RELATIONSHIP BETWEEN MISSION AND OUTCOMES

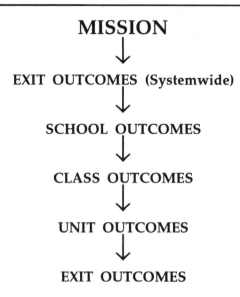

MISSION
↓
EXIT OUTCOMES (Systemwide)
↓
SCHOOL OUTCOMES
↓
CLASS OUTCOMES
↓
UNIT OUTCOMES
↓
EXIT OUTCOMES

Exit outcomes are the result of a consensus of what the finished product should be. Of course, a "finished product" when working with students is approximate. The exit outcomes usually look similar to those listed in Chapter 1.

A random sample of public schools nationwide would produce very similar outcomes. Even though most statements of outcomes would be similar, the process of developing them is an empowering exercise for parents and teachers, and is absolutely essential if the school is to map a strategy for accomplishing its mission. The outcomes listed above would support a mission directed toward learning for all, success for all.

The development of outcomes may lead to the assumption that outcome-based education (O.B.E.) is advocated. O.B.E. is a significant movement in education. In fact, it may be the most viable model of total improvement of schools. An integral part of outcome-based education is the abandonment of the select and sort model of education.

Those interested in improving the schools must look at every vehicle designed for this purpose. As useful as outcome-based education is in promoting change of the entire system of education (this is usually described by the over used term "systemic change"), there are some problematic considerations which must be considered prior to adopting this model.

As outcome-based education has spread, there have been uninformed zealots and proponents of the status quo who have caused controversy and misunderstanding about its value and purpose. Some of the new concepts of organizational change incorporated into outcome-based education fit together like a shiny new car placed in the parking lot of a supermarket. Many who pass admire its beauty, but uninformed and uncaring drivers park along side and knock "dints" in its shiny exterior. Soon those who pass criticize the owner of the vehicle and the vehicle itself.

Part of the problem with the criticism of outcome-based education is based upon the fact that it is perceived as another fad or movement. Its very name "Outcome-Based Education" has become the victim of "handle pathology." Handle pathology occurs when a program, movement, or method becomes widely known and attracts baggage simply due to all the use and misuse of its name by both the informed and uninformed.

Educators typically contribute to "handle pathology." This happens when a new direction, or thrust, is immediately given a label or handle. The label is then used and reused until it begins to represent redundancy and mindlessness. It becomes baggage and harms the very program is represents.

Another problem with O.B.E. is the raft of consultants who have swarmed to this movement as an entrepreneurial activity. To engage knowledgeable consultants can be helpful, but can be expensive. In the end, change in education occurs as a result of the efforts of those working on the front line of the organization. A consultant from outside the organization can be helpful in getting started, but make sure the consultant understands that one of his or her jobs is to help keep cost *down*. Work with the consultant up front and plan for his or her exit.

Another of the consultant's jobs must be to assist in using this model to achieve a paradigm shift. O.B.E. is not a component. If properly implemented, it brings contextual change.

The author recommends the comprehensive knowledge base of outcome-based education as a way of improving education from top to bottom. Taking advantage of the positive aspects of this model without falling prey to the "handle" problem is worth considering.

The following passage shows how controversy can surround a school improvement effort once it becomes identified with a movement or achieves a well-known "handle":

> "Indeed O.B.E. is a wonderful match. In classroom philosophy, it is practically multiculturalism twins. . . . But O.B.E. is just one part of a larger movement in public education that dovetails with the multiculturalists' mission.
>
> Surely there is no grand conspiracy. More likely, educrats just parrot one another's gibberish. But, how is it that so many of the well-heeled foundations, the federally funded regional education labs, the education schools, publishing houses, testing services, and state education departments are singing from the same 'reform' choir book? They are moving virtually in lockstep toward replacing classroom competition (grade structure, objective tests, Carnegie units, ability grouping) with cooperative, feel-good projects that enhance self-esteem. . . . In Pennsylvania, a parents' revolt led to that state's House of Representatives voting 139–61 this month to reject O.B.E."

This quote is from the editorial page of the *Richmond Times Dispatch*.

Let's briefly explain O.B.E.. What are the standard tenets of this school renewal effort?

> *The Vision*—Incorporates some concept of schools becoming learning organizations with identifiable outcomes.
>
> *The Mission*—Contains commitment for all students

to be successful learners.

The Outcomes—Exit outcomes are usually set with broad professional and community consciousness about the skills students should be able to demonstrate upon completing the school or school system.

Progress Outcomes—Learner outcomes are stipulated as progress indicators as the curriculum is designed back from the exit outcomes (in O.B.E. terminology, this is the "design-down" principle).

Other Qualities—

♦ Curriculum alignment in order to make sure the K-12 curriculum leads to the exit outcomes.

♦ An instructional model based upon a variety of knowledge bases, such as TQM, Cooperative Group Learning, Mastery Learning, and Glasser's theories. The focus of the instructional model is always expanded learning opportunities for all students. The outdated teach, test, and grade model is debunked.

♦ The expectancy that all students will become successful learners interprets as the anticipation that achievement will in no way resemble the bell curve.

♦ The management of time emerges as a major concern as time is recognized as a major control variable which schools can use to insure learning for all students.

This thumbnail sketch of O.B.E. shows this process to be a vehicle, not a philosophy. It is obvious that local interests set the outcomes, and from that point O.B.E. is a structure which will help to achieve success.

It is obvious from the brief analysis of O.B.E. that this program is not a curriculum, a religion, or a belief in humanism. It is a vehicle, like a new truck. The old truck will break down or spill its cargo before it reaches the destination. The new truck will deliver its contents to the destination. It's critical to understand that trucks do not determine their cargo.

TRANSFORMATIONAL OUTCOME-BASED EDUCATION

Transformational O.B.E. follows closely the characteristics of O.B.E. as outlined above, except the traditional time constraints of the Carnegie unit are abandoned and the separation of subjects is questioned. The curriculum is reorganized into significant spheres of successful learning and components of the curriculum may be wrapped into a new approach, comprehensively leading to the exit outcomes.

Some form of transformational O.B.E. may be the eventual end for O.B.E., but this approach for most school systems constitutes "loading too much on the plate." It is difficult to change the organization's bell curve and all its vestiges and add to the load a new and more comprehensive approach to the curriculum. This is simply beyond the capacity of many school systems.

If curriculum restructuring around "significant spheres of learning" is desired, a sequential, incremental approach may be useful. Beware: Transformational O.B.E. has the potential to introduce discordance and chaos, resulting in the entire reform process being scuttled.

Ellis and Fouts, in writing a research-based analysis on several educational innovations, devoted a chapter to O.B.E. This is a nice starting place for one who wishes a beginner's explanation of O.B.E. They summed, "Still, we remain convinced that much of what is embedded in outcome-based education is sound. After all, who could find fault with an attempt to clarify the outcomes we seek?" (9)

THE COALITION OF ESSENTIAL SCHOOLS

The Coalition of Essential Schools is a coalition of school and college leaders centered at Brown University. This group is devoted to school improvement and restructuring at the secondary school level. The national RE: Learning Faculty is also located there. The RE: Learning Faculty is described by CES Director Theodore Sizer as a "large team of able leaders experienced in essential schools" (11). These leaders and their districts, and sometimes states, serve as "critical friends" on a sustained basis to schools, districts, and states early in the process of change. Much of the same knowledge base and research employed by O.B.E. is also used by the Coalition of Essential Schools. Either program could be used as a tool for contextual change because each uses the design-down from outcome approach.

In *Horace's School*, Theodore Sizer describes many of the questions and conflicts which arise as a traditional faculty grapples with trying to redesign the high school. Many of the comments and situations depicted are vividly real. Sadly, one can also remember accepting compromises that satisfied tradition and exterior limitations rather than giving students the kind of education they deserved.

Most persons experienced in school reform, redesign, restructuring, and other processes which ultimately mean change, recognize that it is much more difficult for change to occur in high schools than in elementary schools. The reasons for this are numerous, but three appear in most analyses:

♦ Secondary teachers are more subject driven.

♦ The secondary school develops a "living tradition" which resists change.

♦ Teachers are with so many students each day that they don't become student-centered to the extent of elementary teachers.

The Coalition of Essential Schools offers a ready source of assistance. Two very desirable characteristics of the Coalition are: (a) there is no prescriptive method which must be employed, and (b) the values of the community are recognized in the redesign process.

The elements necessary for fleeing the bell curve which are given in the first two chapters of this book are somewhat different from the nine common principles of the Coalition, but they overlap nicely. For example, if the school adopts a vision, mission, and exit outcomes prior to setting progress outcomes, Sizer offers the following advice:

" . . . A school's program presented essentially as what the teachers do is misdirected. A mindful school is clear about what it expects of a student and about how he can exhibit these qualities, just as a mindful student is one who knows where he is going, is deposed to get there, and is gathering the resources, the knowledge, and the skills to make the journey" (12).

It is possible and desirable to measure exit outcomes in terms of qualities that the student exhibits. There are several exhibitions listed in *Horace's School* which serve as excellent examples. One would ask, however, how a student will most appropriately exhibit an identified outcome—the adoption of exhibitions is most effective when the desired outcome is known in advance.

Once the substance of outcomes is identified, constant assessment is a must. Assessment is misinterpreted often. Madelene Hunter's term of "dipsticking" is the kind of assessment which is desired. It can occur at every level. It is not used as a club and can be as simple as, "How are we doing—let's look at the data."

FACING OPPOSITION TO SCHOOL CHANGE

Opposition to school change arises from those who do not understand the change, those who believe that change may diminish a previously existing opportunity, and those who oppose change because it simply creates discomfort. Opposition to change is reduced by communication, involvement, and ownership.

Communication is best when it is two ways. Communication is attempted often as a one way public relations effort. This type of communication has some value, but it is not as effective as the communication which encourages involvement. The first involvement within the context of change should be in the development of a mission. If a mission exists, communication should start with revising the mission, deciding a plan to interpret the mission, or making the mission become a reality.

As work begins, a communications strategy should be developed. Ledell and Arnsparger (13) outlined these purposes for a communications strategy.

♦ Involve a broad range of people in discussions

about the future direction of the school or district

♦ Build understanding and support for restructuring (change)

♦ Develop the abilities of those involved to communicate clearly and concisely about the restructuring efforts

♦ Help those involved anticipate, illuminate, and respond to questions and concerns about restructuring

♦ Build regular reporting of the schools' progress in reaching the goal to improve student performance.

A communications team is helpful. The job of the team is to determine ways to secure broad involvement in communication. It is important to create a continuing dialogue about change. In many communities, the school system is the largest employer. The internal dialogue is extremely important. The team should decide how to communicate with professional and classified employees as well as outside sources.

The classified employee is frequently overlooked, but cafeteria workers, bus drivers, secretaries, and others live in communities throughout the district. Citizens often depend upon these school employees for information. They need to be invited for briefings about change and for input when planning change.

A special group to identify for involvement is the opinion leaders. Opinion leaders are individuals with whom others consult when forming opinions about important community issues. These persons are usually well-informed, and have a broad circle of contacts. They can be civic and church leaders, political workers, office holders, or volunteers. Of course, in this group is the religious right. These groups are becoming more active and can often assist if we make a genuine effort to communicate as the change process is beginning.

A relatively simple way for a communication team to identify opinion leaders is for team members to form a list of those thought to be opinion leaders, and interview these leaders. Ask each to name two persons whose opinion they would seek in trying to decide a complicated community question. A pattern usually develops as some citizens receive several nominations. These persons should be involved in the communication process.

The school, or an individual associated with the change, may come under attack. When this occurs, how we respond will affect the eventual outcome. Focus on the message rather than upon a rebuttal. Ledell and Arnsparger (14) offer these guidelines for maintaining your communications strategy (this study was jointly sponsored with the Educational Commission of the States, the American Association of School Administrators, and The National Association of State Boards of Education):

- Make sure you are clear about issues
- Don't overreact
- Select in advance who your spokesperson will be
- Brief the entire staff
- Prepare a written statement
- Provide an open forum
- Invite the media and others into your school
- Don't be defensive
- Don't allow yourself to be insulted (remain above insult)
- If personal safety becomes an issue, call the police immediately.

The simple acts of talking and listening are most effective for diffusing emotion behind an attack. Attack strategies by pressure groups are usually designed to disrupt or to make you appear to be arrogant, unresponsive, and strident. This tactic supports the maintenance of the high level of emotion needed to sustain the attack and to recruit others. Stick with the facts,and talk with the attackers, continuing to accept them as persons of significance.

When the change process comes into the height of opposition, it seems as though attacks are coming from all quarters. At this time, a change of direction is a tempting option. However, this is a time when renewed commitment will help sustain the effort. Conner (15) offers the following as examples of the commitment needed:

♦ Invest resources to insure the desired outcome

♦ Consistently pursue the goal, even when under stress and with the passage of time

♦ Reject ideas or action plans that promise short-term benefits, but are inconsistent with the overall strategy for the ultimate goal achievement

♦ Stand fast in the face of adversity, remaining determined and focused in the quest for the desired goal.

Apply creativity, ingenuity, and resourcefulness, and consider a compromise to resolve problems or issues that would otherwise block achievement, but maintain the goal.

Commitment will cause those who support change to spend the time, endure difficulty, and devote persistence to accomplish the change. This is why a steady flow of internal and external communication is necessary. It keeps those who are committed focused on the task.

SUMMARY

In this chapter, we discussed methods of reform. The purpose was to enable reformers to keep the concept of reform in perspective and to visualize how some critical components which could not change education in isolation might work together as operational parts of contextual change. The principal of the school must take the initiative in school reform.

The new mission of public education, learning for all students, was described. As the new mission and its implications were discussed, several of the areas of working with children, staff, and parents were mentioned. Areas such as grouping patterns, grading, the use of research, parental involvement, teacher empowerment, and outcomes must be aligned in a manner which abandons the old "select and sort" mission.

Outcomes were listed last among the factors meriting special attention as the school is brought into alignment. This was intentional because all other efforts are effective only to the extent that school becomes a better place for *all* learners. Of course, a careful focus on outcomes validates our efforts.

REFERENCES

1. Thomas R. Guskey, *Implementing Mastery Learning.* Wadsworth Publishing Company, Belmont, CA 94002, pg 6.

2. S. Paul George, *What's the Truth About Teaching and Ability Grouping?* (1988). Teacher Education Resources, University of Florida, P.O. Box 206, Gainesville, FL 32602.

3. Jeannie Oakes, "Teaching In Secondary Schools: A Contextual Perspective." *Educational Psychologist,* Lawrence Erlbaum Associates, pp. 22, 129–153. (Note: Requests for reprints should be sent to Jeannie Oakes, The Rand Corporation, 1700 Main Street, Santa Monica, CA 90401.)

4. Paul George, *How To Untrack Your School.* The Association of Supervision and Curriculum Development, 1250 N. Pitt Street, Arlington, VA 22314–0403.

5. Thomas L. Good and Jere Brophy, *Looking In Classrooms* (4th ed., 1987). Harper & Row, New York, NY 10022, pp. 413–414.

6. *Ibid.,* pg. 416.

7. Robert Lynn Canady and Phyllis Riley Hotchkiss, "It's a Good Score: Just a Bad Grade" (Sept. 1989). *Phi Delta Kappan,* Bloomington, IN 47402, pp. 68–71.

8. Wilma F. Smith and Richard W. Andrews, *Instructional Leadership, How Principals Make a Difference* (1989). The Association for Supervision and Curriculum Development, Alexandria, VA.

9. Cecil T. Daniels, "A Principal's View: Giving Up My Traditionalship" (Sept. 1990). *The School Administrator,* AASA, Arlington, VA 22209.

10. Arthur K. Ellis and Jeffrey T. Fouts, *Research On Educational Innovations* (1993). Eye On Education, Box 388, Princeton Junction, NJ 08550, pp. 89–101.

11. Theodore R. Sizer, *Horace's School; Redesigning The American High School* (1992). Houghton-Mifflin Company, Boston, MA, pg. 212.

12. *Ibid.,* pg. 27.

13. Marjorie Ledell and Arleen Arnsparger, *How to Deal With Community Criticism of School Change* (1993). Association for Supervision and Curriculum Development, 1250 N. Pitt Street, Alexandria, VA 22314, pg. 3.

14. *Ibid.,* pg. 30.

15. Daryl R. Conner, *Managing the Speed of Change: How Resilient Managers Succeed and Prosper When Others Fail* (1993). Villard Books, New York, NY, pg. 147.

3

TEACHER EVALUATION

INTRODUCTION

Almost every institutional practice in public education exemplifies the old select and sort mission of education, including teacher evaluation. There is an effort to standardize evaluation with rating scales. This makes evaluation appear to have validity, but this is not the case. Some teachers are expected to be average, others below average, and others excellent. If one looks at the scatter of ratings, a bell curve could be used to depict the results. One might ask, "How could teachers who are rated in such a manner be expected to rate students differently?" This dilemma must be addressed in an effort to restructure or reform schools.

A primary problem with traditional teacher evaluation is that the substance of evaluation does not relate to anything else which is occurring in the school or school system. Evaluation takes place in isolation because it ostensibly supports the need to hold teachers accountable, and because it is administered to satisfy a number of other political, cultural, and educational purposes. The fact that teachers are evaluated gives some pretense of quality control.

Teacher evaluation should be one of the most important things accomplished in the school, only second to the act of teaching. In this chapter, I discuss how to move teacher evaluation beyond the bell curve, and how to use teacher evaluation to dramatically affect the school improvement process. The case is made that effective teacher evaluation must be used as a tool for school improvement.

EVALUATION:
A SUMMATIVE OR FORMATIVE PROCESS?

THE DIFFERENCE IN FORMATIVE AND SUMMATIVE EVALUATION

There is a serious need to change the system for evaluating teachers as schools are restructured. Studies in human motivation showed more than a decade ago that factors which motivate high performance are to be rarely considered in the typical system of teacher evaluation (1–2). The problem is that motivation may not be viewed generally as a purpose of teacher evaluation. It is, however, a very critical component since teacher evaluation should impact the quality of teaching by inspiring better performance.

A primary question of teacher evaluation is, "How can an administrator serve both the supervisory function and the management function?" In other words, how can an administrator be both helper and judge? (3) This question leads to some new theories about the purpose of evaluation as well as considerations of how the teacher evaluation system can align with the restructured school.

The paradox which arises with "helping and judging" leads to the concept that there are actually two kinds of evaluation which are occurring in most schools. These are usually mixed together in a single effort, and the result is unfavorable. The administrator is confused about his or her role. A question frequently asked is, "Am I seeking to be helpful with suggestions or to be accountable with documentation?" The teacher is confused as well, because the intentions of the administrator are unclear. This leads to the conclusion that there are two separate kinds of evaluation. The helpful, growth directed evaluation is *Formative* evaluation. The administrative quality assurance evaluation is *Summative* evaluation. Each is discussed in the following pages.

In order to make teacher evaluation productive, one needs to understand the implications and uses of both summative and formative evaluation. Failure to establish a clear distinction between the two evaluation strategies and the resulting evaluation protocols creates the conditions for failure of the evaluative process.

Summative evaluation has limited utility for teachers. It is used in an attempt to measure the end product—whether or not the observed teaching meets some preset standard. There is often an attempt to add a formative component by attaching some helpful suggestions. This is a futile exercise because the first critical comment causes sufficient distress to obscure all else.

Formative evaluation is directed toward helping. Formative evaluation is usually not included as a part of the permanent record. It is neither critical nor threatening and does not affect summative decisions such as job retention or tenure. The formative evaluation is usually anecdotal and describes actions observed which demonstrate teaching behaviors previously identified as productive and appropriate

FORMATIVE EVALUATION

Formative evaluation helps to motivate growth. It is a collaborative process, consistent with the concepts of quality, and it assists in exemplifying the mission of success for all— even teachers and others. Arthur Costa outlined the purposes which are consistent with formative evaluation:

> "Imagine a school organization based on the cultural norms of collegiality diversity, creativity, and intellectual challenge; where time is devoted to peer interaction, planning, teaming, and observing each other; where repertoire is enhanced; where intellectual growth is paramount; where teacher participation in making decisions that affect them—curriculum, instruction, materials, staff development, assessment—is valued; where accountability measures and collective evidence of their effectiveness is the responsibility of the staff itself. Perhaps, we need an optimistic reconceptualization of the processes of teacher evaluation to match the re-structured school" (4).

Did Costa paint Utopia? Perhaps not. These are the purposes of formative evaluation. Some of the concepts advocated for formative evaluation in this chapter are unsettling for the administrator who is used to the typical "check sheet" evaluation. But remember our goal: as schools are restructured, we must change perception of the organization and look at *all* our practices in aligning the organization with a new reality.

The concept of formative evaluation can be difficult to comprehend. The following example is useful; the assumption is made that design of appropriate lesson plans is a teacher's action worth observing and reinforcing. An appropriate set of lesson plans might contain several components including these four:

+ A prepared lesson plan was available for the observer.

+ The lesson plan provides a check for understanding.

+ The lesson plan provides extra time for students who do not initially grasp the material.

+ Enrichment activities were planned for those who understand quickly.

These are only four randomly selected components of a satisfactory lesson plan. There might ultimately be as many as 10 or 12 components. In a formative evaluation, the observer of teaching writes specific actions noted as exemplifying each component. As an example, the following is how the first and third components above might appear as documented by an observer:

+ A prepared lesson was available for the observer.
  "The observer was given the outline of a unit plan and a plan for the day upon entering the room."

+ The lesson plan provides extra time for students who do not immediately grasp the material.
  "After the initial exclamation, the plan called for a 'dipstick' activity which was used to assess understanding. This was observed when the teacher gave the group three simple questions, and two students who were having difficulty were pulled aside for individual help while others worked a few examples."

The formative evaluation retains its character throughout—even if a specified component is not observed. There is no criticism; if something is not observed, the instrument is just left blank. It's interesting that a blank "cries out." The observer is almost always asked, "Why is this blank?" A stock answer, "I didn't see that, did I miss it? When can I come back to observe it?" Remember the goal in formative evaluation is to impact upon the future, not to measure the past—thus, the word "formative." The goal of the very brief exercise about lesson plans is not about what should be in an evaluation but to show a simple way to use formative evaluation in a nonthreatening, growth producing manner. This is the meaning of formative evaluation.

Now, the point has been made that there are two kinds of evaluation. Both formative and summative evaluation have a place and value. The problem comes when the two are mixed, and this happens routinely. Some of results of the mixing are:

+ The teacher becomes confused about purposes —"Is this grading or helping?"
+ Formative records are often kept and used as documentation. This makes them summative.
+ Negative comments such as "the room was a little messy for good instruction" kill evaluation as a helpful experience.

Some rules for formative evaluation are:

+ Tenure, retention, and conditions of the job which impact authoritatively upon the teacher are not included in the formative process.
+ Formative evaluations validate those things a teacher does successfully. The entire goal is to help the teacher succeed.
+ The results of formative evaluations are never used in dismissal hearings or in other ways which could negatively impact upon the teacher.

Formative assessment is conducted by the principal, assistant principals, supervisors, department heads, or peers. Of all these, peers may be the most effective assessors. A rule of thumb is that it is very difficult for the formative evaluator to be effective if he or she makes "status decisions," *i.e.*, tenure, retention, and etc.

PEERS AS ASSESSORS

To be effective assessors (note that when formative procedures are used, assessment is the preferred terminology), peers must have effective criteria and receive training in the formative assessor protocol. Peer assessment is such an excellent technique because human beings are motivated to respond to the fulfillment of basic needs. Two or three needs are fulfilled through peer assessments—for instance, the desire to succeed (power) and the need for love (to be respected and esteemed). If there is time for sharing, then the need for fun may also be incorporated into the formative assessment.

The power of what others think, a factor in peer assessment, is illustrated by my own experience:

Once while fishing alone, I lost a large bass which got entangled around the outboard motor. In the melee, it was unnoticed that the old motor had been accidently put into forward gear. Being in a state of disgust for the loss of the morning's only fish, I decided to retire for the day.

When I attempted to crank the motor, it did not start and the pulley seemed difficult. I thought I needed to replace the old clunker as I turned the throttle up and raised slightly to give a hard pull.

The motor started in forward—wide open—and the surprised fisherman went sailing over the stern as the boat without a captain proceeded across the lake. However, the spin of the propeller caused the boat to make a wide turn and head back toward the hapless swimmer.

As the boat approached, I grabbed the bow and became a human rudder. Finally, the motor was stopped in the sand. I climbed aboard, sat stunned on the seat, and did two things I can only hope were accomplished in proper order—I gave a prayer of thanks and looked around to see if anyone was watching.

This true experience is a demonstration of the fact that even in a life-threatening situation, we don't want to appear in a "bad light" in front of those who may, in fact, be strangers. The same psychology at work in the my story works with teachers who wish to appear in a positive manner to their peers.

HOW? WHO? WILL THEY CHEAT?

There are several excellent plans for using peer assessors. One very effective program is to provide peers who are specially trained teachers with released time and a small stipend. The peer observers are then responsible for a number of observations. Typically, a peer observer is responsible for observing six or eight teachers.

Observations can take place during planning and released time. In some school systems, teachers who serve as observers are provided with aides or substitutes. Providing substitutes to allow observations at a time other than during planning period is not extremely expensive. Neither does this take the observer out of the classroom for an excessive amount of time. Possibly a couple of half-days each semester are required for a peer observer responsible for observing six or eight colleagues. If the teacher uses a joint approach with some planning time and some substitute time, missed class time is reduced.

A peer observer who is responsible for observing six or eight teachers can have a difficult time scheduling without some assistance. For example, two observations of about 45 minutes are usually needed for each teacher. An observer may use his or her planning period or there may be a need to observe one or more teachers who are teaching at other times. Some flexibility in scheduling is necessary, and a shrewd building administrator can work with staff to provide this.

A TRAINING PROGRAM FOR PEER OBSERVERS

If peers are to be used as formative assessors, training is necessary, but first one needs an effective assessment instrument. The assessment instrument is a document which describes the observable characteristics of quality teaching. A pertinent question at this point is: "How can quality teaching be truly quantified? Isn't teaching an art?" Yes, teaching is both craft and art, but the effectiveness research has provided tremendous insight into effective teaching since the early '80s. It can now be said that there are certain things characteristic of effective teachers. Effective teachers approach the process of teaching individualistically, but they usually exhibit certain "professional practices" nonetheless.

The identification of valued professional practices for a formative assessment instrument is essential if peer observers are to be utilized. Once the professional practices are identified, peer observers may be trained in the appropriate observation.

The identification of professional practices is a task for research teams composed of teachers and administrators. This practice is consistent with the need for teachers to be realistically involved in decisions which affect their professional lives. The research and study involved in identifying effective teaching also reinforces the goal of decisionmaking based upon research and data. Usually a central "lead" team works to identify a number of professional practices for effective teaching, typically about 10 to 14 practices.

The research units identify several performance indicators or components for each practice. For example, as mentioned earlier, lesson plans are an example of one area which might be considered. A research unit begins by asking, "What are the components of an effective lesson plan?" A tremendous side benefit of developing an assessment instrument in this manner is that those who work with its creation gain ownership as well as additional knowledge about effective instruction. As a result of this process, all teachers begin as peers studying the material to put in the formative instrument. The fact that some later become peer observers is a natural sequence.

Peer evaluators need to become expert in the process of class observation. In the training process, a demonstration lesson is presented, and the peer evaluator does a tandem observation with an experienced observer. A video of an actual lesson is also useful for this purpose. Once the two evaluators have completed observations, they compare notes for consistency.

The training is composed of three parts: (a) peer observers learn what is required to satisfy each professional practice, (b) peer observers learn how to identify components of the professional practices listed in the formative instrument when observing the actual process of teaching, and (c) peer observers learn how to respond to observed needs without being critical. Once a formative evaluation instrument is developed, all members of the administrative and supervisory team must become experts in identifying the teaching behaviors listed. This is necessary because the focus of administration and supervision should be on instruction. They must be knowledgeable about the formative instrument and play a significant role in training observers. Of course, in systems which do not use peer observers, formative observations must be done by certain administrators or supervisory staff members. The following is a discussion from *The Teacher Evaluation Handbook*, showing a possible training model for peer evaluators.

EXPORTING THE TRAINING MODEL

"Once all administrators and supervisors are trained in formative procedures, they can be exported to the peer observers by training units. The training units are now composed of members of the original team which developed the formative instrument and other members of the administrative staff. With both teachers and administrators involved in training peers, the following advantages are realized:

1. Recognizing the expertise of teachers to conduct staff development boosts morale.
2. The trainers have ownership and pride in the system, and these feelings are sensed by the trainees.
3. When an administrator and teacher work together as trainers, each recognizes the competence of the other" (5).

Traditional teacher evaluation with checklists is far from a process to improve teaching; transforming evaluation is a process required if broader based educational transformation is to occur. It is critical that teachers work in teams, that administrators and others be members of those teams, and that any teacher assessments or evaluations support the concept of quality. All the talk of peer training and of using peers as evaluators may be for naught unless the value of this process is recognized. It is disconcerting that a survey by the Educational Research Service indicated that only about 6% of all observations were done by peer observers (6).

USING EVALUATION AS AN APPROPRIATE TOOL

One might ask, "What is the appropriate purpose of evaluation?" These are potential answers:

♦ To foster growth of the classroom teacher

♦ To support the mission of the school system

♦ To assure that teachers are meeting a high standard of performance

The first two purposes are accomplished formatively; the third is accomplished summatively.

> *Very few evaluation systems are designed to support the goals of the school system. This is one of the most serious mistakes for those who wish to reform or restructure education. . . .*

Supporting the goals or outcomes of a school system, and even a new mission, vision, or paradigm, is an important purpose of evaluation. Suppose a school system embarks upon an effort to revise the method of teacher evaluation. The first thought should be concern for using the evaluation system to support the new mission of the schools. The second thought should be for planning the involvement of those to be evaluated.

Revision of the teacher evaluation system should not be attempted until the changes called for in Chapters 1 and 2 are begun. It is only then that this essential ingredient of systemic change can be incorporated. In educational restructuring the entire organization must be coordinated. Total coordination is often referred to as "alignment." In this instance, it is aligning teacher evaluation with the mission and outcomes of the organization. One of the primary concerns expressed in this book is that educators, parents, and others who work with school reform committees connect each component to all other components including a new mission and appropriate outcomes.

CONSTRUCTING THE FORMATIVE EVALUATION SYSTEM

As peer coaches were discussed, some thought was given to designing an evaluation system. We now need to delve deeper into this process. As with most other improvements in education, construction of the evaluation system should be inclusive. Key teachers, administrators, parents, and students should be involved. A critical starting question is, "What do we want in this school system and how should our teacher evaluation system relate to this?"

As an example, return to a familiar theme: "Everyone will be a successful learner!" If this is the mission, some questions come to mind immediately:

- ♦ What teaching practices will be seen if everyone is a successful learner?
- ♦ What are the characteristics of those who are successful learners?

Teachers, students, administrators, and parents should be included in evaluation. Each exhibits certain unique characteristics and a means of evaluating each can be constructed. Teachers are the focus, but formative evaluations for parents are designed by some school systems. They are composed of expectancies for parents and are used to focus upon the actions of the parent which will help the child derive the most benefit from education. Of course, they are self-administered and remain a confidential learning tool to reinforce the efforts of the parent.

To focus on teaching, it is beneficial to look at the unit outcomes. Questions include:

- ♦ How do the unit outcomes relate to course outcomes?

+ Are unit goals clearly articulated?
+ What academic behaviors are observable?
+ How is time managed to assure success?

Many additional questions can be developed, and an excellent formative instrument can be constructed from jointly derived answers. As an example, one of 10 professional practices used by the Orange County (Virginia) Public Schools is included in the Appendix (7).

Notice that each component of the *Professional Practice Instructional Planning* is accompanied by an explanation and a few examples of items the observer might document. Of course, other nonlisted examples which accomplish the component are accepted to leave room for creativity. Also notice that the practice supports the curriculum guides and the curriculum alignment. These in turn support outcomes.

Remember, there are at least four levels of outcomes which will relate to a system of teacher evaluation: systemwide, schoolwide, gradewide, and unit outcomes. All of these are interrelated and mutually supportive.

As with the mission statement, work on outcomes begins by asking and forming consensus on these key questions:

+ What are appropriate exit outcomes?
+ What schoolwide outcomes support exit outcomes?
+ What grade level outcomes are appropriate?
+ What unit outcomes will support grade level outcomes?
+ What benchmarks will be noticed for various outcomes?
+ What are the characteristics of teachers who are succeeding in accomplishing outcomes?

The answers to these questions will eventually lead to curriculum alignment. The concept is to design-back from the exit outcomes. Teacher evaluation should be considered as the outcomes are developed.

SUMMATIVE EVALUATION

As mentioned earlier, the purposes of summative and formative evaluation are so discrete that they cannot be effectively combined into a single instrument; and when this is done, the downside of this practice leads to the conflict described as follows by Gitlin:

> "Much of the argument in this volume has centered on explicating the characteristics, features, and forms of the two antagonistic and competing views of what it means to be involved in evaluation (of teaching, in particular). What we labeled the dominant view was shown to be impregnated with the undisclosed agenda of entrenchment, oppression and submissiveness, and the overwhelming concern to promote only superficial change through ensuring the maintenance of existing exploitative relationships. . . .
>
> The tension between the two major competing paradigms is thus seen to be based largely upon a silent struggle between ideological forces that espouse surveillance, hierarchy and bureaucracy, and the contesting forces of reflection collegiality and educative relations. . . ." (8)

Summative evaluation often falls into the "surveillance bureaucracy" mode. However, it does have some utility, especially if we can realize its limitations and its practical uses.

To assure the public of minimum quality and to document for removing incompetent teachers may truly be the only value of summative evaluation. Some principals who continue to believe in a single "mixed purpose" evaluation argue that this method supports standards of high quality. It's amazing that most politicians and the public in general believe that to "tighten-up" on teachers is an exercise of value. *It is seldom recognized that the teachers are getting about as much learning as could be expected under the present model. Of course, this is the reason a new model is recommended.*

Not more than 2% of teachers are incompetent, and another 5% cannot conduct the class without seeking compliance by "setting up" students (cutting grades, giving pop quizzes, assigning busy work, etc.). These are teachers who have large numbers of students fail classes, who always have large number of students absent and tardy, and whose general classroom atmosphere is one of coercion and conflict.

The 2% who are incompetent can be removed. The 5% with poor performance should be placed in other employment, but until they cross the line into documentable incompetence, the summative instrument is of little value. This indicates that in reality summative instruments are useful as public relations devices and as devices to deal with about 2% of the staff.

Perhaps, there might be another value of summative evaluation—to make the marginal teacher uncomfortable. First, it's critical to remember that this group should be worked with from a formative perspective, and there are literally dozens of things which can be done to help a marginal teacher improve. Finally, should all else fail, teachers whose classrooms are not healthy for students must not be allowed to continue their practice. In truth, having a psychologically unhealthy climate in a classroom is almost impossible to document to an extent supportive of dismissal. However, the summative instrument can be used to create a great deal of discomfort. Occasionally, for the person who is already miserable, additional misery helps to bring about change. He or she will decide to improve, quit, or engage in insubordination, which is a dismissible offense in most states.

The summative instruments most school systems now use are quite adequate. In fact, there are those who believe that most of these instruments are already tools of harassment. Therefore, it is not recommended that summative evaluation be changed as part of the reform effort. Instead, avoid use of summative instruments for formative purposes and involve a broad constituency in developing a separate formative instrument. (For those in need of further review of summative procedures, there is an entire chapter devoted to summative assessment in *The Teacher Evaluation Handbook* (9).)

VIEWING EVALUATION AS PART OF THE CHANGE PROCESS

If success is expected for all learners, teachers are included as very significant learners in the school environment. Teachers must constantly learn and renew. A restructured organization should make decisions based on research and data, and teachers must make daily decisions based on best practice. Best practice is known by assessing results (data) and learning new information (research). In the new organization, the leader must be the one with the knowledge. Teachers can be the leaders within a school by virtue of possessing knowledge. The school principal may be the official leader, but the most successful principals utilize transitional leaders as they emerge with knowledge.

If teachers are to lead, what does this do to the principal's role? He or she facilitates! The sharing of power does not diminish the principal's authority. The focus of the principal's power changes from authoritative allocation to affinitive respect.

Does this advocate that the principal relinquish leadership? Not at all! The principal who shares must be stronger and better informed. The sharing process is usually done through committee work in quality groups. An understanding of total quality management (TQM) would be helpful. I found Betty L. McCormick's book, *Quality and Education: Critical Linkages,* provides actual examples which are helpful (10).

All this relates to teacher evaluation because teacher evaluation must be that part of the restructuring process which reinforces change. Evaluation must help institutionalize any change in the organization. The adage, "that which is evaluated is perceived as important, and that which is important gets evaluated," is very useful.

The proper use of evaluation is rare in many school systems. To reemphasize—the main purpose of teacher evaluation is to improve instruction; however, a significant role of teacher evaluation is also to reinforce organizational change.

NO BELL CURVE FOR TEACHERS

The new expectancy of success for all learners must be exemplified in working with teachers. Expectancy is critical.

The select and sort mentality applied to teachers presumes that about half the teaching force is below average. It's common sense that any group—students, teachers, administrators, etc.— fits this pattern, isn't it? Certainly not! It is actually unethical to accept this perspective as the final word in education.

The expectancy must be that all teachers will perform in an excellent manner. As we have seen, more than 90% already meet this expectancy. If this expectancy of excellence is expressed and demonstrated, those who do not perform in an excellent manner will be more motivated to do so. The purpose of restructuring is to give teachers an organization that will support their ability to perform. The problem with teacher performance is not a teacher problem, it is an organizational problem.

It is now reasonable to ask, how can teachers be expected to abandon the bell curve if they are evaluated in a manner which supports a bell curve mentality? This question requires no answer. The answer is obvious. This question compelled that this chapter on evaluation be included as part of this book.

With the expectancy that all will perform in an excellent manner, a five point scale is not appropriate. Formative evaluation must support high expectancies, so normative evaluations are discouraged.

A plus is that teachers will constantly attempt to meet criteria established in formative processes. This professional pride is a wonderful asset—it helps make change possible. When the appropriate tasks are identified and support is given, teachers will achieve!

HOW DOES EVALUATION FIT INTO THE NEW ORGANIZATION

Figure 3.1 shows how the components of change, including teacher evaluation relate to each other.

The Vision and Mission must be directed toward schools which are different from those conceptualized 50 or 75 years ago. The Outcomes are identified and everything else—research, data, components, and teacher evaluation—supports the Vision and Mission. Notice that teacher evaluation is tied to research, data, and components. It also has a two-way relationship with Outcomes.

FIGURE 3.1 THE RELATIONSHIP BETWEEN COMPONENTS OF CHANGE

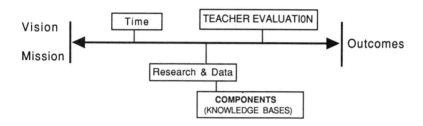

MORE ABOUT THE PHILOSOPHY OF TEACHER EVALUATION

The generally accepted concept is that good teacher evaluation points out some positive things, and provides some constructive criticism. This is common sense taken to the point of ignorance. There is no such thing as constructive criticism!

Talk to a person who has been constructively criticized. Ask them how they feel. One usually hears expressions like betrayed, picked on, hurt, lied to, lied about, misunderstood, criticized by an "incompetent." Years after the constructive criticism, the one who received it can relate the incident and express how they felt about it. By this time, they may have decided that the constructive criticizer was, perhaps, correct; but the negative impact remains. Years later, assessment will also reveal that the positives can't be remembered. Perhaps, there were 10 positive things and one criticism, but invariably the criticism will mask the positive in long-term memory. What is the appropriate way to inform a teacher that something needs improvement, if not through criticism? The same way one informs one's spouse that there is too much garlic in the spaghetti sauce—carefully!

These same concepts were recently expressed and considered with a group of teachers who were members of the local superintendent's advisory council. At first, some were a little skeptical about the despairing remarks concerning "constructive criticism," but after one or two teachers related experiences with traditional evaluation, the group members decided that negative comments by evaluators are basically demoralizing and serve little purpose.

The first story related by a teacher in this group was of her first year evaluation. The assistant principal visited her room and completed an evaluation that "was very unfair." When asked about the contents of the evaluation the reply was, "My shades were crooked and my desk was messy, and that's all." Knowing that this teacher must have received some positive feedback, I was finally able to encourage her to resurrect a vague thought that, "Something nice must have been said, but I don't know why I have forgotten it."

The incident above is a perfect example of the psychological distress created by traditional evaluation. The reaction of the teacher was very similar to those noted by Popham as he attempted to ascertain whether or not principals could carry out both the formative and summative part of evaluation simultaneously:

> "Many administrators who have been thrust into the formative-summative evaluator role will protest that they can, having "earned trust" of their teachers, carry out both teacher evaluation functions simultaneously. They are deluding themselves.
>
> ". . . Even though many principals believe they can, via trusting behavior, be both helper-person and the hatchet-person, such beliefs are mistaken" (11).

It is true that there may be a few evaluators who possess the personal charisma and ability to give "constructive" criticism, in the form of "feedback." Duke and Stiggins suggest that the evaluator must give feedback in a "sensitive, caring, manner" (12). The problem with this is that teachers are usually quite perceptive and will quickly view a bungled attempt at being sensitive and caring as condescending arrogance. The fact is, the downside of criticism makes its productive use very rare.

If an evaluator is not skilled enough to expose a need without the use of criticism, then the need should remain. This is true except for teachers who are harming children and those who are incompetent. Once criticism is ruled out, other more appropriate ways of targeting areas of needed improvement can be developed. One such technique was mentioned earlier: the observer documents just those things observed from a previously prepared list. Anything not documented sends a noncritical message.

Another way to identify an area needing improvement is through the setting of a couple of job targets following an evaluation. A target should be mutually developed. The target will usually emerge at the suggestion of the teacher. Teachers almost always know precisely where additional work is needed.

Targets may also be developed as a result of some skilled questions by the evaluator. For example, suppose an evaluator visits a teacher and finds that the lesson plan is composed of an entire period of teacher performance. The subsequent noncritical evaluation might include the following: "It was noted a lecture was used for this class period. This was an interesting lecture, but the evaluator was unable to comment on several aspects of our criteria for lesson plans. I will need to return— let's discuss the things on this assessment instrument which I will need to observe." Clarifying the aspects of performance expected on the next observation is a way to get at the problem without direct criticism.

A noncritical way to address the same issue is to ask the teacher to explain why the particular technique was employed. The response might be, "This was an introductory lesson," or, "We needed to develop some preliminary knowledge." The evaluator might ask, "What kinds of activities are planned for tomorrow?" The teacher may respond with plans for student involvement. After the observer revisits the classroom and sees student involvement, the response might be, "This plan for student involvement was wonderful. Do you think an introductory lesson might contain a few similar elements?" It is agreed that a new approach will be tried when introducing the next unit and, perhaps, the evaluator will enthusiastically return to observe.

With skill, formative evaluation does not need to incorporate criticism. Why have to overcome a host of negative feelings? The only time that criticism is useful is in summative evaluation, and then only when it is intended to make the teacher feel uncomfortable. Summative evaluation of this manner should be used only when all else has failed. The goal is then to gain compliance, a resignation, or document for dismissal. It is noteworthy that compliance is a hollow victory, but a victory nevertheless, if noncompliance was harming students. Remember, however, that one who is forced to comply will usually sabotage the work group, the evaluator, and the school climate in dozens of ways.

SOME CONSIDERATIONS

It may seem to be evaluative overkill to evaluate teachers formatively and summatively. The thought might be, "There won't be time remaining to do anything else." The time consumed for evaluation should not be a problem because:

♦ A majority of the teachers will not need yearly summative evaluations.

♦ When a teacher is in "need" of a summative process, the entire evaluative protocol becomes summative.

To separate summative evaluation from formative assessments actually frees the school principal and allows him or her to assist, document, encourage, or do other things which will lead to resolution (of one type or another) of the problem of a nonperforming teacher.

For most teachers, the formative process moves forward with instructional improvement as the focus. As mentioned earlier, peers, supervisors, department heads, or assistant principals usually conduct formative assessments.

STRENGTHENING THE PROCESS

A positive way to cause and reward quality instruction is by paying a small stipend to those who perform a high percentage of the indicators listed on the assessment instrument. For example, turn to *Professional Practice No. 3* in the Appendix and review the 11 performance indicators. If a formative observer observes, perhaps, nine or ten of the indicators and documents how they were accomplished, a small stipend could be paid to the teacher. Does a stipend make this a summative process? Yes, unless the following are observed:

♦ Make the stipend small ($75 to $200 seems appropriate) and only formatively observe two or three professional practices per year. Make this a 3- to 5-year cycle to observe between eight and twelve professional practices. Large stipends create anxiety by their very nature. This makes them summative.

♦ Make sure that each observer knows it is a goal for each teacher to be successful and collect the stipend. This means returning to the class to observe any performance indicators not observed the first time. It may even involve finding assistance for the teacher who is not able to demonstrate the required number of performance indicators.

In order to keep the small stipend from appearing to be totally inconsequential, pay for two or three practices simultaneously. Assume the responsibility to help the teacher in whatever way necessary to collect the stipend. This is a formative process, and success is the goal.

Remember, to limit the number who may receive a stipend kills the value of formative assessment because it becomes summative. This is also true of basing a stipend on a one-time observation. In a formative process, we are after growth, and growth comes with guidance, practice, and multiple opportunities. (This is the retest principle applied to teachers.)

This small performance pay system is not a "carrot and stick" approach for teachers. Certainly, teachers will not be motivated significantly or intensively with a small stipend. The value of the plan is to create a reason to focus on growth, cause professionals to work together to improve instruction, and place additional emphasis on formative evaluation.

Finally, a nonperforming or incompetent teacher should be removed from the formative process. The principal should inform the teacher that there are serious problems with performance, enumerate the problems, and place further assessments in the summative realm. This is often known as placing a teacher on a "plan of assistance." In a plan of assistance, the problems are outlined, expectancies are issued, assistance is provided, and evaluation is summative.

Objective observations are used in both the formative and summative processes. The documentation should relate specifically to what is observed, not record broad value judgments such as "Mrs. Smith exhibits a wonderful attitude toward teaching," or "Mr. Smith seems frustrated by the class." Describe specifically observed actions which might lead to those broad judgments.

WHY TYPICAL TEACHER EVALUATION
IS INCONSEQUENTIAL

In the typical school, teacher evaluation is something that happens to teachers once or twice each year. Usually a supervisor or assistant principal comes by and completes a brief observation form. The typical form may include as few as six areas similar to the following:

♦ Professional preparation

♦ Planning

♦ Instruction

♦ Discipline

♦ Personal effect

♦ Administrative duties

Often each area is followed by a blank space for writing the relevant evaluation or five columns to be checked off, headed as follows:

1. Unsatisfactory	2. Needs Improvement	3. Average	4. Above Average	5. Outstanding

If an assistant principal or supervisor does the first evaluation, the school principal usually visits and completes a similar evaluation on the second trip. If the two evaluators agree generally that the teacher is performing at or above the average range, then the year's evaluation is complete. In some schools if either of the evaluators identifies an area in need of improvement, a list of recommendations is developed. In fact, some evaluators believe that they have accomplished their task only if an area for improvement is identified. It is not unusual to hear, "Everyone can improve!" or, "An evaluation is of little value unless a challenge is offered."

A system of evaluation similar to that outlined above is used thousands of times yearly in schools across the United States and Canada. Occasionally, an incompetent is removed with this procedure, but this is rather unusual. There are a few exceptions to the typical procedure just discussed! In some states, as part of the reform movement, complicated and comprehensive evaluation systems have been developed. However, many of them accomplish in a sophisticated fashion no more than the old simple systems. They reflect the same select and sort attitude toward teachers which is endemic in the entire system of education.

Interestingly, there is often a slight departure from the bell curve in teacher evaluation. This is caused by an unwritten accommodation between the teachers and the administration. It is similar to the following—only the most outstanding teachers will receive the top mark (usually a five, an excellent or a superior), most average teachers are rated as above average, and those needing improvement are marked average, areas of unsatisfactory performance are rated as needing improvement. Only gross malpractice is rated as unsatisfactory. The result is a curve which is slightly "skewed" toward the top categories.

This evaluation system, in which most teachers are rated as above average, is an accommodation with an unspoken message which states, "I don't really want to confront you and I'll give you a four on this ridiculous sheet. In turn, you continue to do your job and do not challenge my leadership."

What are other reasons for this unusual accommodation in traditional teacher evaluation? There are at least three: (a) the evaluation does not relate significantly to teaching and the instructional process, (b) the evaluation does not relate to school or system outcomes, and (c) traditional evaluation is mostly a summative process and serves to create an adversarial relationship. Therefore, the sense of the entire process is, "Let's get this thing completed and get on with our work!" It is a hope that some of the concepts offered in this chapter will have two effects: (a) stimulate an interest in additional study of teacher evaluation, and (b) help in building the recognition that in a restructured organization every practice must be scrutinized and aligned.

SUMMARY

An evaluation system which supports the mission of the schools is a critical part of any effort to move beyond the "bell curve." The evaluation system has three purposes: fostering growth, supporting the school mission, and measuring standards for performance. Teacher evaluation has two components—summative and formative. Summative evaluation is used for accountability and formative evaluation is used to promote growth.

It is extremely difficult to combine summative and formative purposes in a single instrument. A combined instrument with "constructive criticism" fails to take advantage of the research on human motivation. A properly designed and utilized formative instrument can bolster teacher morale, build team spirit, and promote quality instruction.

If teachers are expected to abandon the bell curve and all its implications in instruction, then teacher evaluation also should be reconsidered.

The expectancy must be (a) that all teachers are successful learners, and (b) that teacher performance will be competent. Peer observers are must be utilized as a means of improving evaluation and recognizing the professional potential of teachers.

Change involves not only how students are treated, but also how adults in the organization are treated. The teacher evaluation system needs to support and reinforce all other changes in the restructuring of education.

REFERENCES

1. Frederick Herzberg, Bernard Masusner, and Barbara Synderman, *The Motivation To Work* (1959). John Wiley and Sons, Inc., New York, NY.

2. Thomas J. Sergiovanni, "Factors Which Affect Satisfaction And Dissatisfaction in Teaching" (Vol. 5, May 1967). *Journal of Educational Administration*.

3. Robert C. Hawley, *Assessing Teacher Performance* (1982). Educational Research Associates, Anderset, MA, pp. 12–17.

4. Foreword by Art Costa, pg. vii, in Sarah J. Stanley and W. James Popham, *Teacher Evaluation: Six Prescriptions for Success* (1988). Association for Supervision and Curriculum Development.

5. Renfro C. Manning, *The Teacher Evaluation Handbook* (1988). Prentice Hall, Englewood Cliffs, NJ, pp. 66–67.

6. ERS Report, *Teacher Evaluation: Practices and Procedures* (1988). Educational Research Service, 2000 Clarendon Boulevard, Arlington, VA 22201 pg. 5.

7. *Assessment for Professional Development* (1991). Orange County Public Schools, Orange, VA 22960, pp. 23–26.

8. Andrew Gitlin and John Smyth, *Teacher Evaluation: Educative Alternatives* (1989). The Palmer Press, Taylor and Francis, Inc., 242 Chess Street, Philadelphia, PA 19106–1906, pp. 160–161

9. *Ibid.,* pp. 105–121.

10. Betty L. McCormick, *Quality and Education: Critical Linkages* (1993). Eye on Education, Box 388, Princeton, NJ 08550.

11. W. James Popham, in *Teacher Evaluation: Six Prescriptions For Success* (1988). Association for Supervision and Curriculum Development (ASCD), 1250 N. Pitt Street, Alexandria, VA 22314, pg. 59.

12. Daniel L. Duke, Richard J. Stiggins, *Teacher Evaluation: Five Keys to Growth* (1986). A Joint Publication of The American

Association of School Administrators, The National Association of Elementary Administrators, National Association
of Secondary Principal, and The National Education Association, NEA Professional Library, Washington, DC, pg. 32.

4

ATHLETICS AND OTHER SCHOOL ACTIVITIES

INTRODUCTION

One of the first reforms many districts choose when deciding to reform the schools is to restrict student activities, particularly athletics. The mentality which leads to this represents major mistaken assumptions. Actually, if the goal is to have better schools, one should eliminate all restrictions and requirements relating to student activities.

The final sentence in the paragraph above is controversial, but it is truly possible that the reader may come very close to accepting this concept by the end of this chapter. Perhaps, the reader will disagree and "come down" on the side of academics. Let's look at the implications.

THERE IS NO SIDE!

It is amazing that when academicians and practitioners debate student activities there are always those who support a "liberal" view of student activities and those who adhere to an "academic" view. Each view has about the same number of constituents.

In reality, there is *no side*! Those who believe in learning for *all* students soon recognize that academics and student activities are mutually supportive endeavors. We would not think of excluding a student from geometry because he or she can't carry a simple note when trying out for the school's show choir. Conversely, it is no more logical to exclude a student from a competitive show choir because he or she cannot grasp geometric relationships.

It is essential to ask two simple questions—"What do we want?" and, "What will help us get there?" Agreement on the answer is likely to emerge—"success for all students" and "success will breed success."

Geometry is a nice example because it is unique in the math sequence. It is very possible for a student not to possess the learning style required to excel in geometry and yet be quite capable in most other math offerings and in other subjects.

The important lesson here is that everything in the curriculum and everything called *extra* that parallels curriculum has something significant to contribute to the total development of the student. If this were not true, why waste time with them at all?

LOOK AT GOALS!

If the mission is success for all students, it might be helpful to establish some goals which would indicate success. Listed in Figure 4.1 are several typical goals. Beside each goal is a column for academics and a column for activities. The reader is invited to place a checkmark that indicates whether the goal is enhanced most by activities or academics. Make only one mark for each goal or domain. (Activities represent all extracurricular activities, *i.e.*, athletics, music, forensics, Future Farmers, class trips, Future Business Leaders of America, Vocational and Industrial Clubs of America, and others. All of these are activities in which students compete with those of other schools.)

In doing this exercise, what happened? Did you soon withdraw? Did you decide that the author must be "a nut"? Perhaps, you checked some individual goals on both sides even after being instructed otherwise!

I deliberately pulled you into an activity which is basically impossible. It is apparent that neither academics nor activities is the lone source of instruction for most of the goals. This activity simply enforces the view, "There are no sides!"

It is important to remember that those who wish to abandon the bell-shaped curve need to use everything in the educational

FIGURE 4.1 GOAL ENHANCEMENT

	ACADEMICS	GOAL OR DOMAIN	STUDENT ACTIVITIES
A.	_____	Group Cooperation	_____
B.	_____	Responsibility	_____
C.	_____	Skills Development	_____
D.	_____	Goal Setting Skills	_____
E.	_____	Self-discipline	_____
F.	_____	Self-esteem	_____
G.	_____	Academic Information	_____
H.	_____	Physical Development	_____
I.	_____	Development of Talent	_____
J.	_____	Perserverance	_____
K.	_____	Basic Knowledge	_____
L.	_____	Cultural Understanding	_____

arsenal to promote the goals of learning. It is a certainty that various learning approaches and activities are effective for different students, and anything in the school program which will "hook" a student must be available to the educator.

STIMULUS-RESPONSE THEORY IN OPERATION

Unfortunately, when school reform is attempted student activities often become a target, as if these activities detract from learning.

As seen in the preceding exercise, student activities reinforce every worthwhile goal, as does academic work. Actually, academic activities and student activities reinforce each other.

Stimulus-response (S-R) psychology was developed as a tool to explain how learning occurs. The advent of its use parallels roughly that of the bell-shaped curve. As we have seen, there were conditions in society which made the bell-shaped curve have utility.

The S-R theory also had utility. It was an explanation of learning for a time when simple measures and simple techniques were thought to be effective for the "selecting and sorting" responsibility of the schools.

How is S-R theory related to school reform? This antique learning theory continues to drive the decisionmaking of those who create barriers for students. A brief examination of S-R theory is helpful.

S-R theory was used by Ivan Pavlov around the turn of the century in experiments which showed that a dog could be induced to salivate in response to certain stimuli. He extended further his experiments and applied much of his work to human psychology. The great psychologist, B.F. Skinner, developed further S-R theory as applicable to human learning. The process of associating positive or negative occurrences with automatic responses was called conditioning.

Even a casual belief in S-R theory has led to many inappropriate conclusions relative to human behavior. The "if you don't do this, I will do that" mentality, which is seen in everything from state mandates to athletic prohibitions, is a direct and, perhaps, perverse throwback to stimulus-response mentality. Even the concept that failure will provide a stimulus for better performance comes from S-R philosophy.

According to Alfie Kohn, there is almost universal agreement throughout society and its institutions that the reality relative to human motivation and conduct may be interpreted by behaviorism and Skinnerian theory. This accounts for the reliance upon incentives and prohibitions to influence behavior. Focusing on education, he said:

> "For those who look at education from a public policy perspective, issuing reports on American schooling, serving on task forces, or publishing columns, the solution to whatever is wrong with the system invariably

takes the form of some combination of carrots and sticks: Teachers ought to be rewarded or punished for their performance; schools should be threatened with lower enrollment if they do not somehow whip themselves into shape and successfully compete for students. Free-market conservatives, heaping scorn on teachers' unions, or at least their most visible representatives, disagree only about specific policies. On the underlying philosophy, they speak the same language. . . . People respond to incentives. . . . This sort of doctrinal consistency is a rare and extraordinary thing to behold" (1).

The attack of some school reformers upon scholastic athletics provides an excellent example of behaviorism at work. Many states have followed the reformers assumption that "to participate in athletics is a reward." Therefore, according to S-R logic, in order to raise standards schools should hold this reward hostage and, thus, produce results (more learning for more students).

The results are the "No Pass, No Play" mandates of the reform movement in several states, which occurred mainly because politicians don't understand how the mission of education has changed. They feel pressure from all sides that "something isn't working and change is needed." This need for change is often addressed with mandating and posturing. Simple solutions are the favored vehicle for attempting change.

Texas and Virginia serve as interesting examples of S-R policy-making because each took a somewhat different approach but had a similar goal: more learning for students. One common method both states used in the attempt to achieve the goal was to restrict student activities, chiefly athletics.

In Virginia, the State Board of Education created a test of basic competence composed of three subsections—reading, writing, and math. This test, known as the Literacy Passport, is administered for the first time in the sixth grade. Each student in the Commonwealth is required to pass all sections before entering the ninth grade, which is generally considered the first year of high school.

During the first year of testing, superintendents, principals, and teachers began to ask, "What will happen if any students do not pass the test by the time they complete the eighth grade?" At first the answer was, "They can't go to high school." It was soon pointed out that this answer created a real dilemma. To deny students high school entrance would mean increasing the number of overage students, which opposed another state goal to reduce this population. There was also the question of whether the Literacy Passport should cause a student to be retained when the student had legitimately passed the grade.

Finally, after grappling with this problem for almost 3 years, the time for decisionmaking arrived. The first group of test-takers had moved through the system and now was ready to enter high school. It was apparent that about 5% of the students promoted to high school had not passed the Literacy Passport Test.

The State Board of Education then issued a decree, "The students may be placed in the ninth grade, but they can't participate in competitive activities."

Administrators and teachers who understood the negative potential of this Skinnerian mandate pointed out that the few who had not passed the test were largely at-risk students who needed two things: additional time and continuing involvement in student activities. The activities would allow them a measure of success while continuing remedial work.

The policy was defended as responding to political reality— "The public wants school reform, and we have come down on the side of academics."

In Texas House Bill 72, a school reform bill, contained legislation which was known as "No pass, No play." In order for a student to participate in activities, he or she had to pass all subjects.

This bill was passed, in part, as a response to some well publicized abuses in the scholastic football program. Interviews with several Texas school superintendents and Professor Arnold Oakes at Texas A & M University, indicate that HB 72 produced several results counterproductive to the original legislative intent. The situation with football in Texas changed very little because the season was, perhaps, into the sixth or seventh game before the first eligibility period was complete. The student activity hurt most by the legislation was, possibly, Band. The net result of the law was students taking easier courses in order to insure eligibility. This tendency to avoid vigorous courses was cited by Oakes as the most serious problem created by the law.

The "top-down" decisionmaking in both Texas and Virginia demonstrated action in support of an S-R mentality. Each was clearly "if you don't, we will" despite a goal to improve education. In both states, it is commendable that there is an effort to reform education. Creating barriers for students was misguided. This kind of policymaking is like shooting oneself in the proverbial foot.

Efforts at reform in many other states are often directed toward an obsolete paradigm such as, "If we want to improve education, we must measure achievement, then require students and teachers to work harder. We must punish those who don't measure up." Usually, for teachers, punishment is public exposure or mandated "inservice." Students, often lose the privilege to advance or to participate in activities.

States usually measure reform efforts by "objectives" on norm reference tests. In discussing this, Glasser pointed out that this politically motivated measurement accelerated as state departments became threatened due to political pressure for school reform. This entire process was viewed by Glasser as contrary to true reform. The only result of increased testing pressure, however, was to require teachers to teach fragmented facts in an attempt to raise scores (2).

COOPERATIVE GROUP LEARNING

Cooperative group learning was discussed earlier, but it emerges again as a significant concept in activities. Cooperative group learning is a productive strategy to use in the classroom. If one looks at the factors involved in cooperative group learning, it becomes apparent that this is a student activity. The application of cooperative group strategies should be a required base of learning, a performance competency for every teacher if the use of research-based teaching is recognized as important.

It is enlightening that coaches, directors, and sponsors of student activities are often found using cooperative group learning. This is one of the reasons activities are popular with many students.

In preparing for an athletic contest or a band competition, learning must be complete. There is no such thing as receiving a passing grade if 70% of the notes are learned or if 70% of a play is learned. The goal is for all participants to know their parts. Time becomes a controlled variable as all learners must receive the varying amounts of time needed for complete learning. This need for complete learning often leads to a reliance on cooperative groups. Why can't learning in the classroom be approached with the same expectancies for completeness?

It would be unfair or misleading to imply that coaches and directors are more talented than other teachers. As might be expected, some are among the best and others are not. Experienced administrators will recall teachers who approach learning for an activity and learning in the classroom as if each were mutually exclusive. The basketball coach who teaches health and physical education with different techniques than those used in coaching is an example. This demonstrates total failure to make the connection that complete learning is equally involved in the classroom.

Cooperative group activities used by activity directors are called such with some license. Cooperative group procedures may be rendered incomplete because responsibility is not divvied out equally.

It is not atypical to hear something similar to, "Jim, you take the trumpet players to the practice room." "Bill, you go with him and make sure that everyone knows his part." This is not a complete cooperative group activity. Why? Because this is not shared responsibility for the various members of the group. With a little extra training, those who conduct activities could easily spread out student responsibility in group activities. Even though the procedures are approximate, sponsors of activities utilize cooperative groups regularly.

STUDENT NEEDS

As previously discussed, students will work if they perceive an activity to be need fulfilling. All human beings spend their lives in meeting personal needs.

For many students, school is not perceived as a need fulfilling place. If any activity is seen as not fulfilling, then avoidance can take the form of skipping school, sleeping in class, refusing to participate, escaping via alcohol or drugs, etc.

Often if the academic aspect of school is not need fulfilling, an "extracurricular" activity may provide a satisfying outlet for need fulfillment. The student may repress the tendency to engage in negative avoidance activities because he or she finds success in an activity. This is the strongest case for not building barriers for participation in activities.

Notice that in this chapter the term "extracurricular" has been used very sparingly. *Extra* makes this term a misnomer. Like a train, the curriculum runs on two rails, one is academic and the other activity. If one rail is misguided, the train wrecks. Each rail supports learning in a valuable way. Both work together to meet the student needs essential for motivation.

It is an interesting fact that the important role of student activities, particularly sports, is a cultural phenomenon in America. Recently, academicians began to realize the full impact of sport in culture (3). This, perhaps, strengthens the argument that to hold participation hostage to other educational goals is shortsighted, indeed.

Failure to use activities to augment the student need system also can occur at the elementary school level. The following is an example of incorrect use of barriers for an activity:

> A fourth grade class was planning a trip to the Smithsonian Institute as a way to reinforce the study of two units in American History. The teacher prepared a study sheet with questions to be reviewed before departing and questions to be answered upon returning.
>
> As a part of the planned activity, the teacher created barriers for participation. The students were each requir- ed to earn a small amount of money by taking part in class activities such as car washes and bake sales. Students were required to hand in all homework assign- ments and not accumulate over three citizenship demerits for 4 weeks prior to the trip. Citizenship demerits were given for being late to class, being called down in the cafeteria, etc.

A few days prior to the trip, the teacher told four students that they did not qualify for the trip. As a result, two irate parents visited the principal's office and insisted that the students attend.

In discussing the situation with the teacher, the principal was told that the requirements were imposed to teach responsibility to the students who were expected to demonstrate responsibility without prompting from the teacher.

This example should give rise to concern early on because the teacher monopolized the planning. The fun of planning, the challenge of working in groups to create study guides, and the power of setting the requirements for taking the trip would have been ways to provide students with need fulfilling activities.

Of course, barriers should be tied to expectancies, and it should become the teacher's responsibility to assist the students to be certain that enough alternatives were provided to enable expectancies to be met by all. It would, indeed, be inappropriate to allow the four students to miss the trip as it is an important reinforcement of learning.

How did the principal resolve the issue with the protesting parents? In the short-term, she assisted the parents, students, and teacher in negotiating some suitable alternative means for the students to show responsibility. In the long-term, she provided some assistance in planning activities to incorporate the motivational (need fulfilling) aspects.

ACTIVITIES AND ACADEMIC ACHIEVEMENT

It is a fairly widespread belief that student activities, in particular athletics, detract attention from learning, but research disproves this belief.

The most active students have the best achievement records, as shown in at least two action research projects. In one such study, the grade point averages of all the athletes in school were compared with an equal number of randomly selected nonathletes. The grade point average of the athletes was almost five-tenths of a point higher on a four-point scale. In another study analyzing the disciplinary records, it was found that students involved in any kind of student activity were significantly underrepresented.

Other research leads to the conclusion that students of all ability levels achieve at a higher level if they are involved in school activities. Several important findings are cited in support of student activities, as a result of research by the National Federation of State High School Associations (4):

- ◆ Activities support the academic mission of schools
- ◆ Activities are inherently educational
- ◆ Activities foster success in later life
- ◆ Participation in high school activities is a valuable part of the overall high school experience
- ◆ Students who compete in high school activity programs make higher grades and have better attendance
- ◆ Participation in activity programs yields positive results after high school as well
- ◆ From a cost standpoint, activity programs are an exceptional bargain when matched against the overall school district's educational budget
- ◆ Activity programs fulfill students' basic needs, help in students' attitudes toward self and school, and minimize dropout and discipline problems

It is interesting that reformers often attempt to create barriers to athletics in order to enhance achievement. Conversely, some of the well-known prep schools actually require student participation in activities, and some public school systems view athletics and other student activities as part of the curriculum. The examples below are the Woodberry Forest School in Virginia and the Linsley School in West Virginia, and the Henrico County Schools in Virginia.

Woodberry Forest

The Woodberry Forest catalog contains the following:

"Every Woodberry Forest student, regardless of size,

talent, or previous experience in organized sports, spends a portion of each day participating in some phase of the school's athletic program. Therefore, the program meets a broad range of needs.

"Since physical fitness is an important part of an individual's development, the goal of the athletic program is to provide a vigorous, challenging sports program that will help each student develop a strong, agile, and healthy body. Woodberry believes that athletics, properly taught and supervised, can contribute much toward developing confidence, leadership, teamwork, and respect for the rules of fair play. . . . Our coaches emphasize sportsmanship, team play, the development of specific skills, and above all, the true spirit and joy of wholesome competition. Effort in sport is a matter of character rather than reward. It is an end in itself and not a means to an end."

Linsley

At Linsley School, the emphasis is on student activities including athletics. The students are kindly "encouraged" to participate. If a student does not participate, he or she is called into the office for a conference. The net result is a participation rate of almost 100% yearly and 90% participation in any one of the three seasons.

Both of these fine private schools enjoy favorable reputations for their college prep programs and their emphasis on the total development of the individual.

Henrico County Schools

The Henrico County School Division is one of the top school systems in the Commonwealth of Virginia and it ranks among the best in the nation. The leadership in this system views activities as a third curriculum component. According to Henrico, the curriculum contains academic and elective subjects and activities. Many public school systems across the nation take a very similar approach. In fact, this is a special value of public education for many parents. They desire to have a well-rounded program with a multitude of experiences. It is also a desire of many parents to have their children learn to work cooperatively with children from many backgrounds. All this is offered in the public school setting.

STUDENT ACTIVITIES FOR ALL

An attack on the "student couch potato" is underway at Orange County High School in Virginia. Plans are proceeding to require additional activity credits for high school graduation as the school moves to a four-period block schedule.

The concept of activity credits for high school graduation is not new, but it needs a new visit with some timely realizations in mind:

+ The physical condition of today's average student is not as it should be

+ The incidence of mental and physical health problems among students is alarmingly high

+ Volunteerism is a concept which must be taught to students

+ A student who is involved in activities is exposed to opportunities to gain a feeling of self-worth. This actually helps improve grades

The potential activity credit concept at Orange County High School is being considered with the thought that each student should earn activity credits for at least six of the eight high school semesters. It is thought to be inadvisable to require an activity each semester as flexibility for students would be reduced. It is not uncommon for students to start an activity and find it not as originally perceived, so some flexibility is needed.

Activities qualifying for credit include all kinds of volunteer projects plus the traditional activities such as choir, forensics, athletics, etc. Two main concerns are guides for planning:

+ Inclusiveness—Count any activity which meets the intent of the policy. For example, a question came up about horse care, grooming, and showing competitively—when the responsibilities involved with this effort were weighed, of course, it qualified.

♦ Effort—A minimum effort must be required with
each activity, and a method of monitoring must
be set.

The staff at Orange County High School will work through
many questions prior to initiating activity credits. The concept
was explained to parents, and the support for such a program
was surprisingly strong.

ACTIVITIES AT ALL LEVELS ARE IMPORTANT

Even though the emphasis is different from grade to grade,
each level of schooling lends itself well to student activities.
As the needs of students change, so do the nature of activities.

For example, children in the lower elementary grades need
to learn appropriate behaviors for working in groups. Roles
and proper contributing behaviors are important for children
to learn. As cited in an earlier example, a typical mistake is
too much teacher "doing." Teacher doing is different from
teacher directing.

In teacher directing, the teacher decides the units of study
and the activities which will support the skills of the units,
with some student choice in activities. From this point, the
teacher plans the role possibilities for the children. Then, the
teacher and students skillfully put it all together. This is
"directing"!

At the middle school level, building social skills and "finding
oneself" continue to be important. Self-image is so important
at this level. Group activities with alternating leadership are
important. Children should not be competitively eliminated
from activities. This is why intramurals are so important at
the middle school level. Prospect Heights Middle School in
Orange, Virginia, is a nationally recognized middle school.
This school's athletics are as inclusive as possible. For example,
in the football program, a unique fifth quarter is used to prevent cutting any student who wishes to play. After four quarters, all students who have not played or played very little
play the fifth quarter. If the opposing team does not have
students who have not played, the second team plays the fifth
quarter team. The wonderful thing about this arrangement

is that students who have not yet reached their growth spurt or those who have not yet developed coordination participate in a significant way. The coach makes this a "big deal" by making proper reference to the "fifth quarter team," *e.g.*, "Those on the fifth quarter team are the ones who have to play with heart!" As would be anticipated, some students on the fifth quarter team end up being among the best athletes in later years when mother nature allows them to catch up.

A WORD OF CONCERN

Even a "no cut" policy in the middle school is not sufficient to meet the needs of middle school students or even high school students. Earlier it is stated that activities, particularly athletics, provided students a source of recognition. There is a downside to this. Athletics, and to some extent, other activities become the arbitrator of social status.

At the middle school level, students begin to divide themselves into cliques. There's the "in crowd," the "geeks," the "red necks," the "downtown Blacks," the "uptown Blacks," etc. Basically, the "in group" is composed of the athletes and the achievers. The members of this group tend to receive institutional rewards. Most of the other groups receive little recognition. It is difficult for many students to gain the visibility received by members of the "in group" and lack of visibility restricts their ability to move into a prestigious group. If students cannot fulfill needs through outlets provided by school, they will devise other means, such as "rebel" groups and "dress cliques" (*i.e.*, special haircuts for the boys and special makeup for the girls and unique clothes for both boys and girls).

Patterns begun in middle school dictate whether the student will attempt to participate in various kinds of activities in high school. By the high school years, some students have already given up and become members of groups whose activities focus on destructive or nonproductive habits.

It is critical for the school to devise ways to break up exclusive cliques or to, at least, cause students to broaden their scope of associates. Schools must develop activities which hold status value, give participants visibility among peers, and give students with diverse talent a way to showcase those talents.

The example of George will bring back memories of similar experiences in almost every school.

> George was a "nerdy," "bookish" looking young man in his junior year of high school. At the school George attended, a major spring play was a tradition. This was not a typical junior class play, it was "the production." All talent available in the school and the community it served was utilized. There was an orchestra and a choir for support, and the production was usually a musical.
>
> George had never considered being in a play and he did not intend to read for a part. His English teacher decided George should read for a part which fit him to a "T." The teacher convinced (or coerced) George to try out and prepped him in advance. George became an instant success. He found himself acting bold and funny, and even though it was acting he felt bold and funny himself.
>
> During play practice, George confided to a friend that he would not attend the prom because he did not know any girls he could ask. His principal was surprised to see George talking to girls in the hallway after the play. Later George came to the prom!

This true example is shortened and oversimplified, but a small amount of success will give a student the self-confidence necessary for taking a risk such as asking a date to the prom or attempting to make new friends.

The *Harvard Education Letter* (5) describes a program called Magic Me, which intends to involve at-risk students, as follows:

> Magic Me brings together middle school students— most of whom have been identified by their schools as being at-risk—with elderly and disabled residents of nursing homes. The program helps turn kids around, explains its founder, Kathy Levin, because "it's about trust and risk, not just kids and old people."
>
> Students stay in Magic Me from sixth through eighth grade. Once a week they are released from several class periods to travel with group leaders to a nursing home.

There, the group leaders (trained volunteers, usually from local colleges) set up structured activities for the students and residents. These range from arts and crafts projects like making Valentines to more physical pursuits like balloon volleyball or dancing.

"The great things about it," according to Peri Smilow, director of Magic Me in Boston, "is that the kids think they're doing it for the elderly and the elderly think they're doing it for the kids." At first, both groups are nervous, Smilow says, but "no one has to worry about what to say because there's always something to do." Activities are designed for pairs to encourage the forging of close bonds. . . .

As might be expected in a program focusing on at-risk youth, sixth graders chosen for Magic Me have worse feelings about themselves and higher levels of depression than peers not in the program. But a year later nonparticipants report increasingly negative feelings, while students in the program have begun to feel better. It appears that Magic Me may help kids avoid the seventh-grade slump—a nosedive in self-esteem and school success suffered by many young adolescents.

Furthermore, participants show a dramatic increase in school attendance. Smilow suggests a simple explanation: "A lot of these kids have been written off by society. Magic Me makes them feel needed."

What if students were required to achieve a grade point average or have no demerits before participating in Magic Me?

ABUSIVE PRACTICE

When reformers wish to put barriers on activities, such barriers are usually directed toward interscholastic athletics, which are usually competitive and receive media attention. The media attention leads to pressure to succeed and leads to some questionable efforts to avoid barriers.

The pressure to succeed is helpful if it causes the pursuit of excellence. It is harmful if it is allowed to cause abusive practices. To avoid wrongful conduct concerning competitive activities and setting barriers, the commitment of the administration and support of the school board is necessary.

Earlier in this chapter, the reader may have gotten the impression that all barriers are held in disdain, but some barriers are necessary. The purpose of the barrier and its potential for enhancing success is the only useful criteria for judging its applicability. Listed below are barriers which will work and barriers which will not work.

WILL WORK!

♦ Requiring sportsmanship and conduct "as a school representative"

♦ Requiring *reasonable* conduct and scholastic *effort*

♦ Requiring responsibility

WILL NOT WORK!

♦ Mandating above average scholastic achievement

♦ Making minimum standardized test scores or minimum scores on some other performance test a requirement

♦ Creating superficial cut-off grade averages (For example, in Virginia, Band can be a highly competitive activity—to participate a student must be in good standing. Conversely, to be a participant on the girls softball team, a student must take at least five subjects and pass all of them. To hold different criteria for the activities would be questionable.)

Now, abusive practices occur mainly when unreasonable and unrelated barriers are created. For example, suppose a coach sees his most skilled track member disqualified with a 2.4 grade point average when a 2.5 is required. Suppose, further, he sees the JROTC drilling on another field. He recognizes that the JROTC members enjoy different standards. This taxes the coach's sense of fairness. We should not pick certain activities for barriers and leave others barrier-free.

Previously, the supportive role of the administration and school board were cited as necessary if abusive practices are to be avoided. Some practices the administration and school board must deal with swiftly are:

♦ Changing grades and other dishonesty

♦ All types of "coverups," such as protecting an athlete who cuts class.

♦ Physical abuse—such as pushing beyond endurance or playing injured players

♦ Psychological abuse—such as name calling and inappropriate pressure to succeed

♦ Failure to expect appropriate demonstration of responsibility, and failure of the coach to demonstrate character

WHAT IF?

What if the door for activity participation is open, and the role of student activities is recognized? What if there are those who are not professional in following reasonable expectancies? Abusers must be dealt with appropriately and immediately.

This does not require state law. It only requires a school board with high expectancies, and a school board who will protect the administrators when abusers are dealt with. This is difficult when a coach or an activity director develops broad support. This is why expectancies should be put into policy in advance.

SUMMARY

There are two concurrent curricula in operation in the typical public school, academics and activities. Both seek to teach many of the same things. The parallel nature of the two curricula become pronounced in the high school.

An outdated, ineffective way for the school reformer to try to increase achievement is to erect barriers for participation. The "if you don't, I will" mentality is a throwback to S-R theory. Select and sort "bell-shaped" thinking is apparent in this approach. With the S-R approach, it is erroneously assumed that quality is enhanced when those who meet restrictive academic criteria are rewarded by participation in selected activities.

It was shown in this chapter that the interrelatedness of both academics and activities requires a different direction for school reform. The goal is for each student to be successful. Any vehicle in the school program which increases opportunities for success is encouraged.

A very few poor examples of abusive practices, such as failure to require responsibilities of students who are talented in sports, have made it politically attractive to "come down on the side of academics." However, in reality there are no sides. In reality, students who participate in activities tend to succeed academically.

Finally, students achieve who perceive school as a place where needs are fulfilled. Some students, particularly those at-risk, find certain activities to be the need fulfilling part of school. Activities can prove to be the vehicle which keeps them in school.

So many of the attitudes and expectancies sought in the school program are reinforced through activities. Three which appear necessary for the mature individual are:

♦ Productive relationships with others

♦ A sense of success

♦ A sense of responsibility

These three things relate significantly to achievement. Any barriers to a part of schooling which strengthen these characteristics should be viewed with caution.

REFERENCES

1. Alfie Kohn, *Punished By Rewards: The Trouble With Gold Stars, Incentive Plans, A's, Praise, and Other Bribes.* Houghton-Mifflin Co., New York, pg. 143.

2. William Glasser, M.D., *QUALITY SCHOOL: Managing Students Without Coercion* (1990). Harper & Row, Publishers, Inc., 10 East 53rd Street, New York, NY 10022.

3. Michael Oriard, "Sporting With the Gods," in *The Rhetoric of Play and Games in American Culture* (1991). Cambridge Press, New York, NY.

4. *Student Activities—In Support of the Academic Mission of Schools*

(Dec. 1992). A Presentation at National Federation (23rd National Conference) of High School Directors of Athletics. Fairfax County Public Schools, 10700 Page Ave., Fairfax, VA 22030.

5. "Hallways, Lunchrooms, and Football Games: How Schools Help Create Jocks and Burnouts" (May-June 1993). *The Harvard Educational Letter*, Vol. IX. No. 3. Longfellow Hall, Appian Way, Cambridge, MA 02138–3752, pg. 1.

5

CLIMATE AND RESTRUCTURING

INTRODUCTION

School climate encompasses all aspects of the school which raise the spirit of those who work within and patronize the school (for both students and adults to become successful learners). Certainly, curriculum is of critical importance, but climate is the enabler, setting the stage.

School climate is a critical area which affects almost every aspect of schooling. Progress and improvement in climate will be noticed immediately. There are a few characteristics of good climate which show themselves in bold fashion, announcing whether those within the school care for each other, care about their school, attend to details, and take pride in themselves and their work. For this reason, any school reform model must include a climate component.

In many schools, climate has been neglected or attended in a "hit or miss" fashion. Giving it renewed emphasis is one of the most effective ways to bring immediate attention to reforms. An effort to improve climate can be recognized quickly, and this has a positive impact. There are few other educational changes in which efforts are realized immediately. For example, the impact of programmatic changes may not show for a several years.

TWO ASPECTS OF SCHOOL CLIMATE

School climate can be divided into two categories—the psychological climate and the physical climate. Both these elements operate in concert to support the effective school. The reader may believe initially that a focus on physical climate puts too much emphasis on the "superficial" issue of appearance. Hopefully, as we progress, neither aspect of climate will be considered superficial. Each aspect of school climate is discussed in the following pages.

THE PSYCHOLOGICAL CLIMATE

The first aspect of school climate, psychological climate, is critical if the school is to succeed. Admittedly, a distinction between physical and psychological climate is, perhaps, superficial, since both must work together in a properly functioning school. However, in a school involved in the process of renewal, the psychological climate takes on overriding importance. It sets the stage for those in the school, both staff and students, to become productive and to embrace quality as a way of doing business.

An outstanding program, available from the Association for Supervision and Curriculum Development, incorporates many of the aspects of restructuring discussed in this book—*Dimensions of Learning* (1). This program will complement staff efforts to restructure the school. The emphasis of *Dimensions of Learning,* which was prepared cooperatively by the Association for Supervision and Curriculum Development and the Mid-Continent Regional Educational Laboratory, is on the instructional process and student assessment. Five dimensions of learning are identified:

 ♦ Positive attitudes and perception about learning
 ♦ Acquiring and integrating knowledge
 ♦ Extending and refining knowledge
 ♦ Using knowledge meaningfully, and
 ♦ Productive habits of mind.

Of the five dimensions of learning, the habits of mind and

the positive attitudes and perceptions about learning are the two dimensions which relate most to psychological climate—and they are always factors in the learning process. This entire program is built around the theory that the psychological climate of the learner is the door which must be opened—and remain open—if optimum learning is to occur. The following quote from Robert Marzano lends the appropriate focus to psychological climate:

"More recently, psychologists have begun to view classroom climate more as a function of the attitudes and perceptions of the learner than of elements external to the learner. If students have certain attitudes and perceptions, they have a mental climate conducive to learning. If those attitudes and perceptions are not in place, learners have a mental climate not conducive to learning. In general, two types of attitudes and perceptions affect learners' mental climate: a sense of acceptance and a sense of comfort and order" (2).

A positive psychological climate in school means the school is a place where the staff and the students have a sense of acceptance, importance, and control. Perhaps this is best described as a sense of efficacy, which involves the following components:

♦ A belief in the possibility of success
♦ A willingness to set high goals in anticipation of success
♦ A belief in the ability to control the conditions necessary for success

The leader in the school influences the development of efficacy more than any other player. A leader who is accepting and personally secure enough to share leadership is usually a successful builder of efficacy.

Efficacy is described by Fields (3) as, "collectively getting things done." This ability to get things done collectively origi-nates at the local school level. Members of the organization feel that the "locus" of control is with themselves and/or their colleagues in the group, faculty, or unit. Fields offers the following organizational checklist for determining members' locus of control (4):

Organizational Locus of Control Checklist

(Write "yes" or "no" in the blanks)

1. We can do something about most of the problems relative to education at my school. _____

2. Few outside events continually control education performance at my school. _____

3. We have a positive attitude about solving any education problem. _____

4. Educators I work with are involved in solving education problems at all levels. _____

5. We can control most of the elements of education in my school environment. _____

(Note: For this chart, "yes" answers indicate an internal locus of control in your school organization, while "no" answers suggest an external locus of control.)

Of course, efficacy relates significantly to school culture. Saphier and King (5) outline 12 cultural norms which, if present, tend to sustain school improvement efforts. They are:

- Collegiality
- Experimentation
- High expectancies
- Trust and confidence
- Tangible support
- Reaching out to the knowledge base
- Appreciation and recognition
- Caring, celebration, and humor
- Involvement in decision-making
- Protection of what's important

♦ Traditions

♦ Honest, open communication

Saphier and King conclude:

"If we are serious about school improvement and about attracting and retaining talented people to school careers, then our highest priority should be to maintain reward structures that nurture adult growth and sustain the school as an attractive work place. A strong culture is critical in making schools attractive work places" (6).

HUMAN NEEDS AND TEAMS

It is important to review basic human needs in order to understand how these needs might be met within the organization. The two writers most admired by this author in the area of human needs are Abraham Maslow (7) and William Glasser (8). Maslow identified human needs as safety, belonging and love, esteem, and the need for self-actualization. William Glasser identified the basic needs as love, power, fun, freedom, and safety. Any effort to improve or enhance the psychological climate of the school must be built around assisting those in the school to fulfill their personal needs.

In all reality, the essence of a positive school climate is achieved when the fulfillment of personal needs are institutionalized, for example, through such programs as site-based management and quality circles.

Many school restructuring efforts rely on teams to improve the quality of the overall organization and to provide for team member needs. The tasks of restructuring are achieved most effectively if teams are created to assist with various aspects of change. As team members begin to work together, productivity and a sense of achievement (which incorporates several needs) is frequently evident. Usually teams answer three questions as they begin to work:

♦ What do we want to accomplish?

♦ How are we going to tell if we are accomplishing it?

♦ What will the outcome be or what will the situation look like when accomplished?

William Byham, in a little book called *Zapp* (9), described the mutual spark of motivation which people feel when working together to accomplish something worthwhile. He called the process "Zapp." Byham listed the following three functions that channel the effort of a team (with products for business in mind):

♦ **Key Result Area**
  • (The direction we want to go)
  • Example: Increase Output
♦ **Measurement**
  • (A way to know we're moving in the right direction)
  • Example: Number of units moved
♦ **Goal**
  • (Something to tell us if we're there yet)
  • Example: 10% increase

It's amazing how closely the improvement efforts in the private sector mirror those in the education sector. In talking to those working in both, it is notable that members of each assume a unique knowledge base for restructuring their occupation. Both assume their sector is more advanced and informed. Each is surprised to find the other is working from a rather similar research base, which includes organizational improvement and climate issues.

Team efforts should be focused onto the above three areas, but there is a fourth area which should occupy the attention of team members. This is the task of making certain that each team member has the opportunity to contribute significantly.

Making teams a continued part of operation serves two important goals—(a) the accomplishment of a task through the best thinking of team members and (b) meeting the needs of group members in such a way as to enhance the psychological climate of a school. With new teams, there is always some confusion, some false starts, and some uncertainty. The following are ways to encourage new team members and to make sure team meetings are both productive and psychologically enriching.

♦ *Address Purposes*—There is a reason for the change which a team is working on—explain it, and address the expressed fears of the team members. Showing the team members how some of their own needs can be accommodated through this change.

♦ *Give Access*—Support teams and add status to their work by giving them access to leaders high in the organizational hierarchy. For example, suppose some music teachers and the music supervisor are working on a new curriculum. Invite the assistant superintendent to hear progress reports. When work is complete, have the team members meet with the superintendent (in some cases the school board) to explain their work.

♦ *Use Pilot Projects*—A change contemplated by a team seems less permanent and intimidating if it is first structured as a pilot project. Another wonderful thing about pilot projects is that they eliminate much of the fear of failure. It's not uncommon to hear, "This is just a pilot project, if it doesn't work we can adjust it." Because a pilot is not permanent, it offers another advantage—often the change can be tried and proven before harmful resistance gets in the way. Team members working on pilot projects should expand their efforts by communicating problems and resolutions through periodic updates to the rest of the staff.

Once teams are operational and steps have been taken to provide support and encouragement, further organizational skills will help them to be productive. The following are some suggestions offered by Scholtes (10):

♦ *Use Agendas*—After the initial meeting, agendas should be developed by the team. An agenda should include the name of each topic, each presenter, time guidelines, and whether the focus is on information or decision-making.

♦ *Have a Facilitator*—The job of the facilitator is to keep the meeting on task. The team leader may serve initially as the facilitator, but the facilitator's role should be rotated within the team. Other tasks of the facilitator include intervening if team members begin individual fragmented discussions, preventing any one team member from dominating the discussion and assisting the group in reaching closure on each topic. Finally, the facilitator keeps time or appoints a group member to do so. (Note: The most effective meetings are those which have a previously stated ending time. Of course, make it a practice to begin on time. This sets the example for (a) intent of purpose, (b) punctuality, and (c) respect for the time of all concerned.)

♦ *Take Minutes*—Each meeting should have a scribe. Minutes should include main points raised and decisions made. Minutes should be reviewed at the beginning of each meeting.

♦ *Evaluate the Meeting*—Evaluate each meeting and summarize decisions, discussing what can be done to improve the next meeting. A brief evaluation at the end of each meeting helps all team members realize what was accomplished. This is usually more positive than most team members might assume.

♦ *Adhere to the "100 Mile Rule"*—Allow no one to interrupt the meeting to confer with a participant unless the interrupter would have called had the meeting been held 100 hundred miles away. How many of us have tried to participate in meetings only to have one interruption after another? One often wonders if all of these were emergencies.

TEACHER EMPOWERMENT AND SITE-BASED MANAGEMENT

Site-based management was mentioned in Chapter 2 as a change component with promise. Perhaps, the most valuable aspect of site-based management is the support which it lends to a favorable psychological climate in the school. When teachers and other employees within the school are included as decision-makers, empowerment occurs. Many needs are met through empowerment such as power, freedom, and even safety.

Interestingly, researchers have found that schools with a positive climate adopt site-based management more quickly and successfully than schools with a less positive climate. It is also thought that site-based management and teacher empowerment tend to raise morale and positively impact school climate.

An interesting question might be, why initiate site-based management if the school climate is already positive? There are two purposes of site-based management: (a) to improve school climate, and (b) to improve school output. This discussion leads back to earlier chapters because prior to initiating site-based management, leaders should identify the mission of the school and desired student outcomes. This will allow for both the purposes of site-based management to be successful.

Is site-based management a panacea for school climate and school output? Not quite. The research based on the impact of site-based management is not overwhelming. There is a significant difficulty in striking a proper balance between local school discretion and centralized authority. These problems were addressed in an Educational Research Service Report as follows:

"Despite the high expectations held for site-based management, little hard data have been collected about its actual impact on students and teachers, or on the costs and benefits of programs. Indeed, when evaluations have occurred, they have tended to focus on assessing the process of site-base management rather than the outcomes. In part, this can be attributed to the very nature of site-based management. Districts recognize the need for some centralized standards, lest the district become fragmented, and students experience substantial differences in program quality. But if districts demand too much control over each school, the purpose of site-based management will be defeated. Attempting to balance school autonomy with centralized assessment is not easy" (11).

The E.R.S. *Folio* cited as a reference for the quote is an excellent starting point for those interested in beginning an in-depth study of site-based management. It contains an analysis of site-based management and about 40 selected articles on the various aspects of this change component.

Site-based management has potential depending upon the need of each school system and school, but a word of caution is in order—don't try to implement site-based management without extensive study and sufficient time. It appears appropriate to implement site-based management in increments. Certainly, a site-based model implemented incrementally over a period of 3 or 4 years and one tailored to meet local conditions is much preferred to a head-long thrust. Such a move must have a training component for teachers, administrators, and parents, and the strong support of the school board.

Perhaps the most pressing question is how extensive can site-based management become? Most site-based programs will never be able to escape state laws, state board regulations, and various compliance and monitoring mandates. In recognition of this, a list of a few areas of control which can be site-based and those which should remain centralized might be helpful.

♦ Centralized
  • Overall mission and outcomes
  • Hiring policy, *i.e.,* minority and sex equity, etc.
  • Overall budgetary authority and accounting
  • Systematic maintenance operations, such as roofing and other major repairs which require overall planning or long-term co-ordination
  • Capital improvement planning and compliance in such areas as the American Disabilities Act

- System-wide accountability, *i.e.,* test administration and reporting, and various state reporting requirements
- Central purchasing, *e.g.,* paper products, paint, and other items used in large quantity
- Staff development classes to which support the mission such as those on T.Q.M. or cooperative learning
- Personnel functions for allocating and paying bus drivers, custodians, secretaries, and other classified workers.
- Contract administration, *e.g.,* insurance, energy consumption, asbestos removal, and various service and maintenance contracts.

♦ Site-based

- Monitoring and accountability. In any quality operation, frequent measurement and evaluations are critical. In site-based operations, this is usually performed by quality groups. Central outcomes are set, but the local school team decides on complementary local level outcomes
- Scheduling. This includes decisions about the daily schedule. For example, in the high school a staff might decide to operate a four-period day or some other schedule modification
- The allocation of the school budget. In a site-based operation, each school is given an instructional budget. Usually, the development and expenditure of this budget is done through team planning
- Reporting to parents and other instructional decisions. The method of reporting to parents is controversial because parents tend to expect letter grades, but it needs to reflect the uniqueness of the school program

- Planning for improvement. An example would be a plan for accomplishing the mission or even expanding upon the mission. There is always the need to look at outcomes and possibly expand them, and there is always the need to ask, "How are we doing?"

- Personnel evaluations. Evaluation becomes real if it belongs to those on the site. (Site-based management is an excellent structure for implementing the evaluation strategies recommended in Chapter 3)

- Setting priorities for maintenance and capital outlay. Even though the maintenance program and the capital outlay program are managed centrally, priorities can be set in the school. For example, which is more critical—the purchase of several desktops, or a new a file cabinet for each teacher? Which needs maintenance priority—the leaky roof or the wornout air conditioners? Priorities could be set at the school level

- Personnel Selection (within district parameters). Districtwide agenda and the individual school needs can be met simultaneously. For example, if a balanced staff is a district goal, then the district can send to the school team only applicants who tend to complement this need. Also school level decisionmaking can remain quite broad—it can involve deciding (a) who is the most appropriate candidate and (b) who would not be appropriate under any circumstances.

A review of the items best left at the division level and those appropriate for a site-based program will leave the astute reader recognizing that all the school-site activities can be initiated without adoption of a site-based program. Indeed, a modified site-based program may be the most desirable solution. Many of the considerations of site-based management which are designed to empower employees can be adapted to other structures whether or not site-based management is adopted. Remember the two purposes of site-based management: school output improvement and a better psychological climate.

Both purposes for adopting a site-based program are interdependent. Unlike other productive enterprises, schools embody an ethos of moral and ethical commitment. If ethos is coupled with intentionality, there is a thrust for quality which will invariably make a productive school.

Attending to the moral climate of a school is another aspect of school climate. The moral climate relates so dramatically to the psychological climate that the author wonders if a clear distinction could or should be drawn. Later we discuss moral issues in going beyond the bell curve.

OTHER PSYCHOLOGICAL CONSIDERATIONS

The psychological aspect of school climate is wrapped in the simplicity and complexity of human need fulfillment. An organization which demonstrates the ability to focus on work and need fulfillment simultaneously is an organization with a good climate.

Some managers are people persons, and they know how to work with groups and individuals intuitively. But even the intuitive people can learn from studying how groups function.

RECOGNITION

Recognition is, perhaps, the most effective tool for enhancing school climate. Those who work in the schools belong to a social-psychological system which is built upon making a contribution to society, and recognizing the individual for quality work satisfies a host of basic needs. The positive motivation which comes from recognition is well-documented by educational research. Recognition motivates achievement for teachers, principals, and superintendents, as well.

Some ways of enhancing recognition are:

♦ Encourage work in study groups or quality teams, building in recognition of success along lines previously discussed

♦ Send teachers a note of appreciation on their birthdays, making it personal and recognizing some special characteristics

♦ Give teachers special recognition during National Teacher's Week and on other special occasions

♦ Write special notes of recognition following any activity sponsored, planned, chaperoned, etc.

♦ Quote positively, *i.e.*, "Last week *(teacher's name)* and I were talking and she/he said _____. I have thought of that since, and I believe we can build upon it." This is called a third person referral. It is effective if spoken in the presence of the teacher or to one or several others who will relay the quote

♦ Arrange special periodic snacks and refreshments to recognize teachers at special milestones, *e.g.*, end of the grading period, completing the yearly testing program, etc. Resourceful principals are able to find sponsors for such activities

♦ Be present at all types of school events, and follow-up with a note to teachers who were present and those working with the activities

In reality, recognition is observing who contributes in literally hundreds of ways in the school and saying "thank you" simply or in some unique way. It's impossible for an administrator or a parent support team to notice everything; therefore, ask one or two trusty allies to assist in reminding you what to recognize. There are others who respond equally to recognition—custodians, bus drivers, cafeteria workers, teacher aides, students, etc. Have you ever seen the reaction of a custodian when presented with a big red valentine by a couple of primary school children? Yes, perhaps recognition is the most positive tool for building climate.

CREATING A POSITIVE CLIMATE—THE STUDENT EMPHASIS

The axiom, "happy students means happy parents" is true to a large extent. If that were changed to "unhappy," it would be even more true. At any rate, educators should direct actions toward enhancing the climate for students.

The classroom is the primary environment for the student, and this is the place to begin climate efforts. As with teachers and parents, there is a physical and psychological climate.

The physical climate for the student starts with the classroom. It should be inviting, displays up, and bulletin boards utilizing bright colors should be displayed with action items appropriate for the age level of students as well as things of appropriate academic interest.

There should be special places in the elementary classroom like a special place to read silently and a special place to do enrichment activities. Creativity is the word here. I thought I had seen special centers created for just about everything, but the dash and seat of a '57 Chevy being used as a fifth grade activity center was most amazing. A folder of enrichment activities was in the glove compartment. Students could sit on the big seat and read or write.

The psychological aspect of climate for students involves fairness and genuine concern. Students of all ages respond to high expectations applied equitably. Teachers should assume a personal responsibility in assisting all students to at least meet the minimal level set.

The psychological climate for students is seriously damaged when teachers use obsolete practices such as teach, test, and grade. Such a procedure leaves a substantial number of students with incomplete learning because there is no preassessment, no formative assessment, and neither reteaching nor enrichment.

Success is the key for an appropriate climate for students. Success begins with students understanding what they are expected to learn and why it is important. The climate for students continues to improve as various research-based techniques such as "whole brain" instruction and cooperative learning are employed.

Finally, any discussion of school climate would be incomplete without mention of the work of Dr. William W. Purkey (12), a professor of education at the University of North Carolina at Greensboro and cofounder of the International Alliance for Invitational Education. Much of Dr. Purkey's work concerns making the school inviting. Of course, the relationship to school climate is obvious. Those who wish to improve school climate should make themselves familiar with Dr. Purkey's work. Dr. Purkey's concept of invitational learning includes many actions which are uniquely human and demonstrate a sense of caring in the school environment. Only a couple of Dr. Purkey's 80+ publications are listed in the bibliography, but this will suffice to get started.

THE PHYSICAL CLIMATE

The physical climate involves aspects of the school environment which are readily observable. It involves the appearance of the building and even to some extent the appearance of those in the building. For experienced administrators, this discussion about physical climate may seem redundant and simplistic, but my visits to many schools have convinced me that the simple tasks of physical climate need to be reconsidered.

When entering a school building, it takes less than 60 seconds to form a first impression. First impressions may be tentative, but they are strong, and things which confirm those initial impressions may be noticed more than contradictory information.

Because of the importance of first impressions, consideration of the physical climate should begin prior to entering a building. Is there visitor parking clearly marked and in a favorable place for entering the front of the building? Visitor parking signs can say much—they can contain school slogans and school symbols or a welcome message. Those who wish to project pride or hospitality are careful to seize every opportunity. Even in an urban area, don't allow signs designed to protect students to send a poor message. Take appropriate steps to protect students, but continue to attend to the message the community receives.

The appearance of the school campus is another first

impression opportunity. The basics of appearance are trimmed grass and bushes, and a few well-placed flower beds in summer. The summer period is a frequent problem for a school campus. Grass soon gets out of control, bushes grow uncontrollably, and the school takes on an unattended appearance. If the principal and secretary are out of the school for most of the summer, provisions can be made to secure volunteers or funds to get these jobs accomplished.

The problems of summer occur because of a failure to recognize the importance of climate. The school principal gets priorities out of sequence, for understandable reasons. The principal is oriented toward the inside of the building. It is important to get the school ready for the children and teachers. There is scheduling and curriculum work, and there are hundreds of interruptions. Among the interruptions are interviews with new teachers and enrollment of new students.

New teachers and new students are some of the reasons why attention to the campus is so important. The parents of that new student, or the new teacher who visits, see the campus first. If we have taken advantage of opportunities for a positive first impression, the tone is set for the other expectations which come later.

There should be a sequence to summer work, and the accomplishments of summer should start prior to school dismissal in the spring. Let's discuss the priorities of summer.

When school is out, the first priority must be the campus or school grounds—begin the summer by cleaning the outside of the building: see that grass is trimmed, fix signs, trim around curbs, attend flowers, do minor paint touch-ups, and make sure that the front doors are pleasant in appearance. Typically, the school has four or six front doors, and only one is open—don't make guests guess. Put a sign on the front door which is open, or open all of them.

The reader from schools located where security is a necessity may have to do some improvising and a little creative thinking to make the school appear inviting. There are some urban schools which are both inviting and secure. A couple of progressive companies who are defense contractors make visitors feel welcome and important even with the maintenance of both security and confidentiality. Signs are marked clearly for visitors, identification badges are issued with a welcoming message, and escorts are provided. The escort is there to manage the visitor; however, this is done in such a positive way that the visitor may believe the escort is a personal tour guide.

In preparing the school, make certain the exterior is neat and welcoming before moving to the inside. Clean the entrance lobby first by stripping the floors and waxing them. Throw out spindly interior plants and get new ones, if possible. Remove every box and all other paraphernalia of summer. Typically, the summer cleaning program in the school begins in the classrooms, or with one of the building wings. The lobby is used as a reception area for supplies for the ensuing year. Therefore, visitors to the building must navigate between boxes of toilet tissue and new shipments of textbooks. Find another unloading area. Replace all burned out lights and clean the reception area.

Clean the main office next, and place appropriate symbols on the secretary's desk and the principal's desk. What are "symbols"? They are items which show interest in the level of education which characterizes the school. For children, items on display which are age-appropriate help to create a friendly atmosphere. For high school students, other symbols such as the school mascot and pictures of student academic and sport activities would project the school as a caring place which is "with it."

Do not allow the lobby and main office to become a "summer casualty." In many schools, cleaning the lobby, principal's office, and attending to the outside are tasks saved until just before school starts. The goal is to have them in good condition for the start of school. Perhaps, it's desirable from the perspective of climate to imagine that school begins during summer vacation in those critical areas.

I was recently the guest of a school board in a school district in an adjoining state. It was mid-summer. In our incidental discussions, the school board members were anxious to show off a relatively new school which had been adopted by a local industry. This same school had received some extra state funds, and was unusually well-equipped.

During a visit to the school, I formed a very strong first impression. We approached the school from the side in order to view a special kindergarten playground which employees of the local industry had built. It was enclosed with a 3- or 4-foot chain-linked fence. The playground was wonderful, but the fence had been ridden over by older students in several places and was an eyesore. A top rail would have prevented damage once it began to occur, but a new fence was now needed.

As we drove to the front of the school, the grass was mowed, but there had been no trimming, and grass was growing through and above some of the shrubs. As we entered the school, an automatic door closure that had become loose was holding one of the doors ajar.

Once inside, we stumbled over a recent shipment of supplies, a handcart, and a scrubbing machine in the lobby. The school office had a carpet with a seam which was pulling apart, and on it sat a huge box of clothes with a sign asking "Are any of these yours?" Apparently it had been sitting there since before school was out. The first impression was already formed.

We met the school principal, who wore a tee shirt, shorts, and tennis shoes. He immediately apologized for the appearance of the school, and said, "It will be shiny when the students arrive—we are in the middle of summer cleaning." As we toured the remainder of the school with the principal, his knowledge of the program and love of children began to overcome the first impression.

Wouldn't it have been possible to attend to most of the first impression problems as soon as school dismissed for the summer? This takes just a little focus on school climate.

What about the principal's appearance? Was the principal's dress appropriate? Possibly, for local custom, but appropriate casual dress usually includes a collared shirt, trousers, and leisure shoes. It may appear petty to even mention dress of the school principal, but, in a larger context, attention to detail, even personal appearance, makes a statement about focus and approach to our business.

Appearance of the school building as one enters also is of particular importance. Other things to look for in the entrance, as well as the remainder of the school, are: wax build-up next to the wall, broken or dirty windows, and spotted ceiling tile—a particular eyesore. Ceiling tile spots and stains are caused by water which comes from one or two sources—condensation on pipes and/or roof damage. Any temporary roof repairs are likely to last only a few months at most. Condensation can be corrected by wrapping the pipes with insulation or spraying them with foam.

Ceiling tile can be painted if new tile is not available, "but, a leak will just stain them again, so what's the use?" Don't be defeated by a leak! It's true that some leaks on a flat roof seem to defy permanent repair because of expansion and contraction of the building. There are many different solutions for those determined to succeed. I know of one school where sealant is removed and replaced routinely over an expansion problem. There is another where a small piece of plastic is suspended between the roof and the ceiling tile. It catches a small quantity of water which evaporates. This is not an appropriate way to fix a leak, but the principal contends it has saved the ceiling tile for several years.

Many in the business sector have realized the value of physical climate both for boosting employee motivation and contributing to customer satisfaction. The penchant for maintenance and cleanliness at Disney World and the special greeter assigned to the entrance areas of Wal-Mart stores are just two of many examples of attention to the climate which is so obvious in the business world.

Another example of attention to physical climate occurred at a recent professional golf classic. There was a host tent which was for employees and V.I.P.'s of the sponsoring corporation. However, it was also used to contribute to the climate of festivity. A corporate flag flew at every peak and valley of the tent, as well as on the bleachers and at the sky box tent. All the bleachers had been moved in by truck and had probably been scarred in transport, but they looked new because the installer had brought touch-up paint. In a conversation with the installer of seating regarding this and several other examples of attention to climate which had been noted, he said, "Repeat business is less expensive to get than new business. Therefore, we go out of our way to show the customer that we are a quality outfit." Wouldn't we want each of our schools described as a "quality outfit"?

From a teacher's perspective, an important aspect of physical climate is that everything works. It is frustrating for the teacher to have a pencil sharpener which is broken, a computer which has crashed, or a limping chair. Small things can gain a large focus if not attended to. In the school where climate is important, there are set procedures for checking each room and for checking all equipment on a periodic basis.

Once, while I was observing a teacher who was using the overhead projector with a very artful flair in a "brainstorming" session with a secondary social studies class, the back of the overhead popped and the screen was dark. I could sense the frustration as she said to the class, "We will try to use the board." Suddenly, as if a brilliant idea had occurred, she walked to the overhead, opened a small door, took out the dead bulb, replaced it with a spare from the same compartment, and proceeded with the activity.

In discussing this after the class, she related that the blown bulb almost "panicked me . . . but I remembered our conversation in principal's advisory about such occasions, and Mr. Howard (the principal) promised to see that there were always extra bulbs with the projectors."

This experience showed a focus on business. This was advance preparation for an emergency which could have been disconcerting to the teacher. This is a factor of school climate.

STUDENTS

The school and classroom climate are critical for student learning. Students must feel comfortable, accepted, and enthusiastic for optimum learning to occur. The school contributes to this by having attractive bulletin boards which enhance school spirit and which display student work. Some schools are dominated by a concern for neatness to the extent that very little student work is displayed. On the other hand, in some schools the displaying of student work is "junky," with so much work hanging in every configuration that it has no meaning. Tasteful and balanced display of students' best work is the most meaningful approach.

Every school should have a large mirror. Above the mirror should be an appropriate slogan such as, "There's nobody just like me!," or "Pride in myself and pride in my school." In secondary schools, it could be something similar which stresses positive self-concept or achievement. Students enjoy seeing themselves in the mirror, and this can be turned into a boost to climate.

Another "spirit building" activity is to have students paint the school's bulletin boards. Have them painted with the school logo or other subjects of interest to the students. When there is nothing displayed, the board itself then becomes a student display. This makes the school more attractive, because there is nothing uglier than an uncovered bulletin board.

Schools are notoriously drab places, and they get junky as the school year progresses; thus, the need for a schoolwide spring cleaning. Every school needs plants; but as mentioned, plants must be maintained or they become a problem. In one elementary school, cartoon characters larger than life have been painted on 4' x 8' boards and hung in the cafeteria. In another, a local artist has painted a beautiful mural depicting students at play and work. These and other efforts make schools human places, lift the spirits of both students and teachers, and also demonstrate that those in the building are serious about the business of education.

SUMMARY

In creating a school for all learners and going beyond the bell curve, climate is a school improvement component which will make an immediate difference.

Earlier we discussed the necessity of restructuring most schools. The traditional school embraced the assumption that the bell curve was an appropriate tool for viewing the achievement of students. To move away from this concept, a contextual change (a change which affects the very core assumptions upon which the organization functions) and some component changes (surface changes which may augment achievement) work in concert.

An improved climate is a wonderful component change.

It signals a seriousness of purpose which can be viewed or felt immediately. An improvement in climate makes a statement that, "This change process is real." The quick results which can be achieved will attract attention immediately and set the stage for other changes.

Those who are associated with a church or synagogue recognize that religious organizations have long known the value of symbols as catalysts for deep change. In education, climate can serve as such a symbol.

Two types of climate were discussed—the physical climate and the psychological climate. The psychological climate is necessary to build a sense of ownership and appreciation for achievement among both adults and students. The physical climate can be used to project a seriousness for the business of education and to project a penchant for detail. A prerequisite for developing the ethical organization is to pay attention to climate.

REFERENCES

1. Robert J. Marzano, Debra J. Pickering, Larry E. Arredondo, Guy J. Blackburn, Ronald S. Brandt, and Cerylle A. Moffett, *Dimensions of Learning* (1991). Association for Supervision and Curriculum Development and Mid-Continent Regional Educational Laboratory, ASCD, 1250 N. Pitt Street, Alexandria, VA 22314.

2. Robert J. Marzano, *A Different Kind of Classroom: Teaching With Dimensions of Learning* (1992). Association for Supervision and Curriculum Development, 1250 N. Pitt Street, Alexandria, VA 22314, pg. 20.

3. Joseph C. Fields, "Unlocking the Paralysis of Will" (June 1993). *The School Administrator,* American Association of School Administrators, 1801 N. Moore Street, Arlington, VA 22209, pg. 9.

4. *Ibid.,* pg. 10.

5. Jon Saphier and Matthew King, "Good Seeds Grow in Strong Cultures" (1985). *Educational Leadership,* Association For Supervision and Curriculum Development (ASCD), 1250 N. Pitt Street, Alexandria, VA 22314, pg. 67.

6. *Ibid.,* pg. 74.

7. Aberham H. Maslow, *Motivation and Personality* (2nd ed., 1970). Harper and Row, New York, NY, pp. 38–58.

8. William Glasser, *The Quality School—Managing Students Without Coercion* (1990). Harper and Row, New York, NY, pg. 49.

9. William C. Byham with Jeff Cox, *ZAPP: The Lightning of Empowerment* (1992). Harmony Books, New York, NY, pg. 11.

10. Peter R. Scholtes and others, *The Team Handbook: How to Use Teams to Improve Quality* (1991). Joiner Associates, Box 5445, Madison, WI 53705–0445.

11. Educational Research Service, *Folio on Site-Based Management*, 200 Clarendon Blvd., Arlington, VA 22201.

12. William W. Purkey, *What is Invitational Education?* (1990). International Alliance for Invitational Education Publication, 349 Curry Bldg., University of North Carolina, Greensboro, NC 27412–5001 (PH: 919–334–5100, ext. 69).

    William W. Purkey and P.W. Stanley, *What Office Professional Can Do to Make Their School "The Most Inviting Place in Town"* (1990). International Alliance for Invitational Education Publication, 349 Curry Bldg., University of North Carolina, Greensboro, NC 27412–5001 (PH: 919–334–5100, ext. 69).

6

ETHICAL CONSIDERATIONS

INTRODUCTION

Even if a school's belief system is not transmitted to students explicitly, it is transmitted implicitly. It is an ethical decision to consider surpassing the bell curve as a mission. Conversely, both to adhere to the select and sort model and to deny that "all students can be successful learners" have ethical implications. The effort to restructure schools must have an ethical base.

The First Amendment to the United States Constitution was designed to insure certain basic, personal freedoms or civil rights. It reads:

> Congress shall make no law respecting an establishment of religion, or prohibiting the free exercise thereof; or abridging the freedom of speech, or of the press; or of the right of the people peaceably to assemble, and to petition the Government for a redress of grievances.

This Amendment is among the most important amendments, if not the most important. Simply recall the history books filled with graphic descriptions of how one government after another, armed with the correct "word," wreaked carnage on nonbelievers.

Having given the First Amendment its due, it is appropriate to point out that while the establishment of religion by government is prohibited, in the same sentence freedom of speech is guaranteed. At times, these rights and prohibitions clash head-long and find controversial ground in the public schools.

The First Amendment must be respected and upheld, but this in no way requires the public school to abandon the responsibility of becoming an ethical institution. Yes, it is of foremost importance that schools maintain neutrality with respect to religious indoctrination; but one must recognize that religion is not the only institution which has ethical or moral responsibility. In fact, one wonders how or why these ethics and morals have been interpreted as belonging to organized religion.

There are ethical considerations which impact upon professional persons in interactions with students, parents, and other public school constituencies. These matters interlock with the contextual and component considerations for school restructuring. Sergiovanni shared a similar view:

"We need to be in touch with our basic values and with our connections to others. In other words, we must become more authentic with ourselves and others. If we are successful, we will be able to transform schools from ordinary organizations into learning communities. But success will mean seeking new bases of authority for leadership. Bureaucratic and psychological leadership are not enough. Our goal should be to develop a leadership practice based on professional and moral authority" (1).

Some ethical aspects of change and their implications for improving the public schools need to be addressed. As the chapter progresses, it becomes apparent that an important ethical responsibility of the school is to enable students to function economically in mainstream society.

PREPARATION FOR CITIZENSHIP AND OBTAINING CULTURAL KNOWLEDGE

The importance of a broad access to knowledge is more pronounced than in the past. One of the primary ethical considerations is that the school help all students have equal opportunity to obtain knowledge. Basic cultural understandings should be a part of this knowledge base as a powerful and enabling force. The increasing rate of enrollment of students who speak a primary language other than English, is a graphic reason why the expansion of cultural knowledge has become critical.

Two well-known writers, Bloom (2) and Hirsch (3), have aptly explained the importance of cultural knowledge to forging a coherent society in the United States. Hirsch wrote from the perspective of the public school student and Bloom wrote about the college student. Both writers decry the lack of a common knowledge base among our future citizens. Such a common knowledge base includes ethical concepts. While the author's concepts for the instructional program and curriculum would differ considerably from Bloom's and Hirsch's, both make valid points about the need for a common culture.

The Federal Government is an unintentional or unwitting contributor to the deculturing of society. The creation of protected minorities who have special rights has had a divisive effect upon society. While positive action was necessary to assure civil rights, an unintended side effect was movement away from the common culture as a societal goal. The "melting pot" concept does not appear politically correct to advocate, but the thrust for separatism moves people away from the common culture to the separate subculture. This tends to isolate subgroup members from the larger society, diminishing many opportunities which are available to those in the mainstream.

Another way the Federal Government contributes to the deculturation of society is by relinquishing control of immigration. As a result of such policy (an unannounced policy, but a policy nonetheless), some central cities seem like foreign countries. The schools are overburdened to an extent that the load of diversity may prevent effective acculturation. Again, this has a diminishing effect upon opportunities for subgroup members.

The public school's role in assuring that all students are successful is a role necessary for society and the individual. The school must help the minority student to be able to function smoothly in the subculture and in mainstream society. This includes allowing the student's need to belong to be fulfilled by the subculture and the student's economic need be fulfilled by mainstream life. The education required for this task is an extra burden on the school and the student in many instances. It requires becoming bicultural and bilingual.

I write of subculture and its limitations with personal knowledge. Having come from a closed culture deep in Appalachia, I found my native speech and expressions to be quite limiting in mainstream society. In college, a favored professor advised, "You must become bilingual with the use of a single language." I realized I needed to change my dialect, diction, and usage. Once I did, at least to the degree possible, there was some subgroup harassment whenever I returned to Appalachia. This happens to an even greater extent with a completely different language or race.

An ethical responsibility of the school is to train future citizens to be American citizens first. It is also an ethical responsibility to respect the subculture of minority groups. These two responsibilities appear to clash, but they must be combined and form one of the primary points of focus for the school and the teachers. To address both needs requires school sensitivity and teachers' caring and concern. Failure to address this ethical responsibility has these consequences:

♦ Students will exit school without the skills to function in the larger society and without the skills necessary to adapt to the continuous change they will experience as citizens and economic participants in our society

♦ Students might be forced to choose between the basic culture of the minority group and the culture of mainstream society. A choice of this type involves the possibility of estrangement from friends and family or a loss of the potential to function fully in society—in most cases this carries a rather significant economic and personal cost

Why do the teachers and the school get stuck with this ethical responsibility? Mainly because despite the problems often attributed to public education, the teacher and school represent the most stable and long-term institution available to address this problem. In the past, too many students from subcultures have been allowed to languish until they eventually became dropouts. A salient reason for restructuring is to create conditions in which these students can be successful.

The discussions of ethical responsibility and the teacher begs another question: Why is teaching considered an ethical act?

TEACHING—AN ETHICAL ACT

During the last 50 years, educators have claimed professional status on the basis of the unique science and technology of teaching. After the "effectiveness" studies were disseminated broadly in the early '80s, the fervor for professionalism became even greater. There appeared to be a much stronger scientific and technological research base tied to effective practice.

Even with scientific research that validated effective teaching practices, a strong detractor from professionalism remained: the fact that a few exceptional persons can walk in "off the street" and successfully teach a class of students. Such persons may never have taken a teaching course or had any teacher preparation.

The example cited above is a relatively rare phenomenon, but most experienced educators have seen it occur. The point is, science and technology within themselves will never bring professionalism to teaching.

It, then, becomes obvious that two additional components must be added to research when discussing teaching as a profession. These constitute the ethical components, and they arise from two perspectives:

♦ Commitment

♦ Allocative Responsibility

An ethical commitment occurs when members of a group decide to devote their very "being" to the service of others. This commitment is what differentiates the professional teacher from the educated person who may be able to teach, not certification. The effort to assign teaching professionalism on the basis of credentials and preparation is a part of the technological approach to professionalism, which has not worked well because it ignores ethics. Political control of the technological base has suppressed the full development of an ethically-based profession controlled by its members—such as that observed in accounting, law, or medicine. Commitment coupled with a system of professional ethics and augmented by a strong research base is slowly transferring teaching into a real profession. An important part of this process, from a political perspective, is for certification and licensure to be the responsibility of an independent, professionally constituted board. (Such legislation passed the Virginia General Assembly, but was subsequently vetoed.)

The allocative responsibility of teaching is an aspect of teaching that allows teachers to achieve a greater depth of professionalism—it is the most powerful tool of the teacher. As the mission of education is expanded to make learning for all children an operational reality, teachers also must address allocative responsibility in a professional manner.

For example, under the select and sort model teachers were often in the position of allocating learning in terms of "who"— Who would be the learners who received high expectancies? Who would be with the slow group? Who would be in an accelerated group? Who would ultimately drop out and who would be leaders? With the new mission, teachers expand "who" and make allocative decisions relative to "what." Critical allocative decisions will be made around time. The primary question of the teacher might be: What can I do to allocate time in a manner which will allow all students to learn? Time and its appropriate use in an expanded "who" broadens the ethical decisions of allocation.

It is now possible to consider teaching as a profession due to three perspectives which combine to elevate the status of teaching: (a) science and technology, (b) commitment, and (c) expanded allocative responsibility.

THE ETHICAL VALUES WHICH A PUBLIC SCHOOL MUST TEACH

Whenever ethics are discussed in education, someone asks "whose ethics?" This question leads to endless debate. There are, however, primary values which are central to the very existence of society, including:

- ◆ Honesty
- ◆ Commitment
- ◆ Respect
- ◆ Responsibility

There are other ethical considerations for which you might argue successfully, but most will relate in one way or another to these primary areas. For example, some might say that discipline is an ethical responsibility of the school. Discipline is important, but the acceptance of *responsibility* for one's actions is the ultimate goal of discipline.

There are literally dozens of ways that these primary concepts can be taught. They were woven into books and stories which children often used in school several years ago. Then, there was the attempt to ensure that educational material was not offensive to anyone. Such an effort, taken to the extreme, created bland and valueless material. Now, efforts are underway to create materials which reinforce the primary concepts.

Many citizens complain that religion has been taken from the schools. Even infrequent religious expressions such as graduation prayers have been excluded, and this gives rise to further concern. As stated earlier, the basic ethical concepts are not religious tenets; they are interwoven into the creeds of diverse religions as well as successful nonreligious organizations.

A costly mistake is made when we assume that schools should only teach "facts" in order to avoid religion. Students should have multiple opportunities to learn honesty, commitment, respect, and responsibility. As discussed throughout this book, the process of setting a vision, establishing a mission, stating a belief system, and establishing outcomes or standards is critical. This process should be guided throughout by basic ethical considerations. Each is discussed only briefly in the following pages, but the consideration of these concepts is significant if school restructuring efforts are to be successful.

HONESTY

Honesty must begin with honesty to oneself. A standard of honesty, which includes honesty to oneself and others, should be clearly included in a school's code of ethics. Expectancy for honest relationships should start with the school's staff and expand to the school community. Honesty encompasses interpersonal relationships in the business of education throughout the school environment.

COMMITMENT

Commitment includes doing things which are difficult because they contribute to accomplishing the task or to promoting the welfare of the group. It also relates to the ability to see a project through to completion.

The concept of commitment is vital for a productive school. It extends from the school staff to the students; when those in the organization feel individual and organizational commitment, the organization is productive. The effort of each individual is expanded and reinforced when there is a sense of organizational commitment. Students and staff members work as a team with a spirit which overcomes extraneous detractors. This was stated somewhat differently by Sergiovanni:

> "It is no secret that the norms of the student subculture can often force students to behave in ways that they might not choose otherwise. Black students who study are often punished by their peers for acting "White"—being "cool" means fast lane engagement in sex, drinking, and so on. It's okay to make the grade by charm, but if you use your brains, you are a "nerd." Social contacts, linked to purposing, are powerful tools for establishing within the school a norm system that is more powerful than the one associated with the student subculture. Once in place, this norm can be a safe haven that enables students to be themselves. It becomes okay to cooperate, to study, to be civil, and so on. . . ." (4)

RESPECT

The term respect may sound curious or, perhaps, repugnant to those involved in the various independence movements which stress a "loosening of conventions" for subgroups seeking various rights or entitlements. Those movements often teach a hostile attitude which views "respect" with suspicion. This is unfortunate because the hostility represents a negative way to secure commitment.

True respect begins with self. It involves holding oneself with a regard which renders self-degradation a very unlikely possibility. Self-respect engenders respect to others, including holding others and their property with a caring regard. A school faculty should address the questions, "What is respect in this school?" and "How is it exhibited by students, teachers, administrators, and parents?"

As the concept of respect is extended to the school as an organization, a pertinent question for all is, "How do my actions demonstrate respect or the absence of respect?" For example, how could a student who is disturbing others respond positively to this question, or how could a teacher answer this positively if he or she had rudely berated a child for not attending to the task at hand?

RESPONSIBILITY

Responsibility in the school setting is usually interpreted in terms of discipline, but the ultimate goal of discipline is to assume responsibility for one's own actions. In addition to discipline, another key area of responsibility, which is important for both the school and the world of work, is learning to be responsible so as to be where one is supposed to be—on time. Responsibility also means extending genuine effort to assigned tasks.

Responsibility in schooling also applies equally to the adults —educators and parents. For example, few would disagree that teachers, administrators, and parents must share in the responsibility of assuring that the school is a place of learning for all students. Adults teach ethical concepts whether or not they intend to. In fact, Ravitch believes example is the most important teacher:

> "The rules of the school affect character by establishing what is permitted, encouraged, or forbidden; adults in the school affect character by the example of their behavior in dealing with students and their colleagues;

the social climate of the school sends clear messages to children about the kinds of values that are prized by students and adults. . . . Values like responsibility, honesty, fairness, independence, kindness, courtesy, diligence, persistence, and self-discipline are not taught by role-playing games; they are taught by the life that is actually lived in the school: by the interactions between adults and children, by the examples that adults set, and by the expectations that are created for students in performing their daily tasks" (5).

If teaching by example works, then what about example and intention? By combining the two through developing covenantal relationships and belief systems, our efforts may be doubly effective.

THE "COVENANTAL" SCHOOL

A covenantal school is a school which has a set of basic beliefs that creates a common bond among the members of the organization. The basic set of beliefs is undergirded strongly by an ethical code. Sergiovanni (6) used the family unit as an example of a covenantal organization. The family unit shares a set of common beliefs directed toward unity of purpose. The covenantal relationship shared by family members results in those who are willing to endure discomfort for the benefit of others because of accepted group beliefs.

All schools are organizations, but some schools are both an organization and a covenantal community. Schools in neighborhoods where the expectancy might not be for achievement can overcome low expectations because of a covenantal relationship with students. Covenantal communities achieve cohesion and overcome such negative influences as cliques and gangs—which will inevitably fill the void if the school is not a covenantal community. How then can a school become a covenantal community?

BECOMING A SCHOOL COVENANTAL COMMUNITY

One of the first steps is for those in the school to adopt a central belief system. This is achieved in a variety of ways, accidental or intentional. A covenantal belief system is composed of a point of reference—a yardstick for interpreting reality. For example, "Around here, we believe it important that everyone be treated equitably." The reference system is composed of shared belief, and shared purposes.

Often some unique characteristics or set of characteristics become the rallying point for developing the organizational reality. For example, school excellence in activities such as athletics or performing arts may become the catalyst. The catalyst alone is usually not sufficient to build a sense of commitment, but it extends and blends into the belief system of a school.

If a belief system is in place, each successful event can be a point of reinforcement which will allow organizational identity building. The following example illustrates this point.

Middle School #3 is in an urban area. After studying effective organizations during the summer, Principal Janet Long and the teacher advisory committee decided that the ethos of the school should be directed toward establishing a caring community. They understood from their studies the importance of creating a covenantal organization. They had begun the previous year with a broadly developed code of ethics, which was now hanging on the wall, but something more was needed.

The code of ethics was not called a belief statement, but was a "who we are" statement with a solid ethical base. Long and her staff believed that the school could be changed in a very positive way if somehow those in the school could adopt the belief system as a personal guide to life within the school. (They were seeking a paradigm change as discussed in Chapter 1.)

They developed a comprehensive plan with the involvement of other faculty members, the parent advisory group, and the students. A description of some of the actions they planned and implemented are:

♦ At a faculty meeting, the members of the advisory council conducted small group meetings to build consensus and to discuss using the belief system as a "yardstick" for measuring the appropriateness of future decisions.

♦ At the next PTA meeting, a program was
  conducted by three teachers. They explained to
  parents how the school was attempting to opera-
  tionalize the belief system which parents had
  jointly adopted in the prior year.

♦ Teachers began to discuss with their classes the
  meaning and implication of the belief system.

♦ At a school assembly, student leaders discussed
  "how our belief system can improve our schools"
  and "things I have seen in school which support
  our belief system."

♦ Weekly, a student would select one of the aspects
  of the belief system and discuss either its meaning
  or some ideas for implementing it. (This was a
  very effective 3-minute piece included with the
  daily announcements.)

Many additional ideas were developed by the faculty as
the year progressed. The continuing catalyst for these ideas
was a group evaluation session where the guiding question
was, "What's our progress in making our school a caring
community which is governed by our belief system?" By mid-
year, Principal Long reported that staff members thought that
progress was being made; however, the first valid realization
came in April when she noticed that no paper towel holder
had been replaced since February. Before, vandalization of
paper towel holders in the boys' restroom appeared to be the
school's unofficial sport. Principal Long had routinely replaced
two or three holders per month. To her, the fact that towel
holders were lasting was a sure sign that ownership of the
school's belief system, which addressed responsibility to the
school, was beginning to show.

A BELIEF SYSTEM OR A CODE OF ETHICS:
A NECESSITY FOR RESTRUCTURING

One might ask whether a school should adopt a belief
system or a code of ethics. Either is appropriate. A belief system

or statement is preferred because it can incorporate ethical expectancies and more comprehensive statements about students, teachers, parents, responsibility to the school, responsibility to each other, etc. Once a belief system is adopted, it has the potential to affect the entire organization. The power of a belief system or code of ethics was illustrated by Hugh Sockett, in discussing the application of a belief system or code of ethics, for the American Psychological Association:

♦ In formal instructional settings and informal contexts with students

♦ In collegial relationships within school

♦ In formal and information relations with parents and other appropriate clients

♦ In management relations

♦ With the discipline to which they have allegiance, a discipline that is itself a living community of scholars with its own traditions (7)

Regardless of whether a school adopts a belief system or a code of ethics, various constituencies should give it life, not just hang it on the wall. Principal Long and her staff made that decision, and an interesting thing happened: the faculty soon realized that the instruction model—which was basically teach, review, test, and grade with a few component innovations —was not consistent with the belief system of the school. There were too many learning failures and too many instances where instruction proceeded without further provisions to assist those who had not learned the material. This realization led to further change.

(For clarification, incomplete learning is a companion of the teach, review, test, and grade technique. This is because a number of students usually make low grades which indicates that learning is incomplete, but they are given the low grade and a new unit is begun. As a result, these students get further and further behind.)

WHAT COMES FIRST WHEN ATTEMPTING TO RESTRUCTURE A SCHOOL?

Earlier we discussed developing a mission and changing the paradigm. This sequence is not the only way to begin contextual change. In the case of Principal Long and the faculty of Middle School #3, the need for restructuring was recognized as a result of trying to make the school a caring community.

Regardless of the path of change or restructuring, ethical considerations must enter the process. For too long, educators have assumed a position of neutrality to the peril of their own organization and profession. Ethical considerations are the very basics upon which public education was built. It's true that religious indoctrination must and should be left to the home and church; but to give up the ethical bases and the responsibility to teach ethical behavior is a failure to understand the meaning of the First Amendment or the ethical purposes of education.

DEVELOPING A BELIEF SYSTEM

Developing a belief system can be approached similarly to any other successful group effort in the school. A representative committee might be appointed to develop procedures and ideals, and draft concepts. There should be a mechanism through which to share information with all constituent groups. The goal must be three-fold: (a) to develop the belief system, (b) to obtain the broadest consensus and ownership, and (c) to have the belief system officially approved at the school board level.

The importance of school board approval must be emphasized. This is critical because conflicts may arise, and in order for supportive decisions to come, the school board must have ownership in the belief system. If the school board is not supportive of the belief system, a valuable partner might be lost should conflict arise. Ultimately, conflicts must be mediated, and the school board can lend valuable support to the process. The productive goal is to have no winners or losers, but to emerge with a belief system intact with a broad base of support.

In the school system where I work, the administrative team (which included the central office staff and the school principals) began a training program which led to the adoption of an innovative mastery learning program. Included in this program were ethical understandings concerning the proper treatment of students.

The School Board was informed and received a training session or two during the first 3 years of implementation. The Board viewed the program as an effort to help a larger number of students to learn effectively. The Board was not involved in any team building or consensus building, and was not asked to adopt a policy or statement in support of this new direction —this proved to be a costly mistake.

Teachers had been heavily involved for about 3 years, but in the third year of the program there remained a few "holdouts." In the view of those who had adopted the program, the "holdouts" were hurting students. The situation finally came to a confrontation over three issues:

♦ *Prohibition of pop quizzes*—These were being used as a tool for control by a few teachers. For example, a noisy class might receive a pop quiz and the grade recorded as a summative grade.

♦ *Prohibition of the giving of zeros and averaging in the grade*—An example was a teacher who gave an assignment and announced, "Everyone who does not get this assignment in gets a zero." (An average student cannot overcome a zero in a grading period.)

♦ *Requiring teachers to make retesting available as part of the instructional model*—There were rules and guidelines to prevent abuse, but when a student wanted to take a retest the teacher would assign work to do as a demonstration of readiness, then a retest was made available. The goal was complete learning.

Some teachers were refusing to follow the new paradigm or to adhere to guidelines relative to these issues. The principals, supported by the central office staff, were insisting upon compliance. Some of the teachers in question knew school board members, particularly one very traditional member. At the next board meeting, he guided the Board in a vote to allow pop quizzes as an acceptable instructional technique.

Fortunately, the other two areas were supported by the Board, but this vote cost the time required to rebuild consensus among the Board, and it hurt the progress of the program. Additionally, it cost an otherwise excellent board member the respect of those who supported the program and understood the ethical issues which were at stake.

Perhaps this could have been avoided if the school board had been involved in a realistic manner as the program was being developed.

The lesson implied by this example was learned. Since then, the professional staff of the Orange County Schools, with the involvement of all stakeholders including the school board, has developed a belief system which includes what we believe about students and teachers (see Appendix).

Some initial questions in developing a belief system include:

♦ Who will be mentioned specifically, *e.g.*, students, parents—or will the belief system be all encompassing?

♦ What groups should be represented?

♦ When does the work of the committee end?

♦ How will input be gathered?

♦ What basic ethics are to become the core of the belief system?

♦ What will be the procedure for adoption?

♦ How will the belief system be published and disseminated?

There is a tendency to avoid the development of a belief system for fear of inciting opposition from conservative religious groups and others. If members of such groups are involved up front, the possibility of this occurring is reduced greatly. In reality, one of the primary concerns of conservative groups is that schools have gone too far in trying to achieve neutrality and in the process have left out significant ethical concepts.

School systems which find themselves in conflict with conservatives can usually trace the problem to a failure to communicate. Many times such problems are the result of actions or programs being interpreted as something not intended; however, after conflict breaks out, it is particularly difficult to explain what was intended. Communications up front and realistic involvement are the key to avoiding divisive conflict. Conservatives are often opposed to the mandated teaching of "values," but clarification of terms and intention usually reveals that "values" in this context refers to several controversial concepts which are in dispute within society at large. The ethical considerations of honesty, commitment, respect, responsibility, and the need to make teaching an ethical profession are usually valued by conservative groups if motives are clearly articulated through appropriate communication.

THE ALLOCATIVE RESPONSIBILITY REACHES BEYOND THE CLASSROOM

Earlier the allocative nature of public education was discussed, specifically implying the making of decisions as to "who will receive what." The very concept of "surpassing the bell curve" cuts to the core of the school's allocative procedures. Thus far, the allocative process has been discussed as a classroom issue. The teacher does make daily decisions which are allocative, but this responsibility extends to the entire school.

Teachers and administrators have a very significant allocative role in making decisions about homogeneous grouping and tracking. Such allocative decisions about group placements affect the future quality of teachers a student is likely to have, the nature of his or her future course content, and, possibly, even his or her future occupation. All this gives allocative decisions high ethical consequences. Placement in an average or lower level homogeneous group should carry due process protections stronger than special education placement because the consequences may be greater. Yet, the former is done with impunity and often without consulting parents or explaining to them the implication of such decisions.

Another aspect of the allocative process in public education which has ethical consequences is equity. This term is frequently used in education and government circles to imply a funding process which insures equal educational opportunities for all students. Because the funding of public education is a local, state, and Federal proposition, the pursuit of equity is illusive. It is nonetheless essential if the allocative aspect of schooling is to be achieved in an ethical manner.

There are schools and school systems where the funding is so insufficient that decisions are focused on toilet tissue and paper towels, upgrading the classroom lighting or buying reference books. In these systems, quality is more of concept than a reality. Of course, there are a few citadels of learning which exist despite such bleak circumstances, but they are the exception. The opportunities offered in other more affluent schools are massive by comparison. For example, up-to-date technology; reading, math, music, and art specialists; diverse foreign languages; multiple advanced placement programs; and science labs which rival some college facilities.

Why must the neighborhood in which a student lives dictate the quality of education received? Many among us prefer not to contemplate this problem. "It has always been that way, and it is difficult to change the status quo," is an often heard response! The stubbornness of the status quo is shown by the fact that change has been virtually impossible except when mandated by the courts. There are about 40 states which have had or are in the process of having equity suits.

Margolis and Moses viewed the pursuit of equity as an issue with great potential for creating unrest:

> "Educational reformers place goals of equality and equity at the top of their hierarchy of values, arguing that it is the responsibility of society to redistribute resources to enlarge educational opportunity for those who are less fortunate. This entails conflict with the interests of those who benefit from the existing situation. Resources are always limited and attempts to increase assistance to one group will be resisted by others who fear less attention will be given to their needs.
>
> "Equality cannot be attained through good intentions. The struggle can only succeed under conditions of strain and challenge to the social and political system. Those

who seek equality do so out of a conviction that it represents a prime social value and reflects the highest level of social justice and morality. However, the more intensely equality is pursued, the more disruptive will be the consequences" (8).

Few localities have the resources to emerge from an inequitable educational situation; only the state can muster the resources to solve the problem of inequity. Most state formulas for financing schools just beat around the bushes of providing an equitable educational opportunity for all students. Many finance formulas are outdated and rely on such factors as income and property values for providing some equalization of state funding, but they do not take into sufficient account three critical factors:

- The unique financial need of certain populations of students. These students might not receive equal educational.opportunity even if expenditures are equal.
- A part of most state formulas relies on local expenditures to round out the needed funding. Many school systems in which unequal opportunities exist could not possibly raise the resources required even if the commitment was there to do so. The vehicles of raising local funds are property tax, sales tax, and various service fees. If local property is poor, sales low, and services meager, the fund-raising possibilities are bleak.
- Inner cities suffer from "municipal overburden." This evolves because the central city has to offer a much greater level of social services than the suburban neighbor, due to the unique needs of the central population. This burden drains funding away from education.

There are bright spots, however. Court cases on school funding inequity have been successful more often than not, and there is a growing consciousness that something must be done. Such consciousness will help with the political aspect of this problem. Finally, the Federal Government appears inclined to revisit inequities resulting from federal distribution of funds.

It's difficult for educators in affluent or modestly affluent school districts to advocate equity of funding, because equity usually means redistributing resources. The result of such redistribution is unlikely to yield enough funding to significantly help poor districts, but it will be felt significantly by the affluent districts because they are usually small in number. This quandary is one which state legislatures must address. The appropriate way to handle this problem is to allocate funds in a manner which does not take funds from the more affluent districts, but helps bridge the gap for poor districts. This approach helps to avoid "leveling down."

In working with the funding issue, it is critical that the state require maintenance of local effort. Many times, poor districts will reduce local efforts unless state law prevents them because they feel the financial problem in all areas—education, social services, and other services such as police and fire protection.

Educators have an ethical responsibility to assist in informing the public of the need for equity. This is an area which requires a united effort. We must ask educators in affluent districts to take a "statesman-like" attitude toward helping a broader constituency so that resources are made available to solve the problems of inequity.

SUMMARY

In this chapter, a some of the issues arising from the ethical responsibility of educators were discussed. The concept of the school as an ethical institution was explained. The importance of schools becoming covenantal communities and some of the opportunities this presents were described. A covenantal relationship within a school appears to make a big difference and is a characteristic often found in successful schools.

The sense of a covenantal community arises from a commonly held set of beliefs. The development of a school belief system is a natural, essential part of the school restructuring process. An example illustrated how one school used its belief statement as a "back door" approach to begin contextual change.

The very act of teaching is described as an ethical activity. The chapter described the ethical nature of the allocative decisions which teachers make, and how their misuse in the sorting of children highlights the need to move "beyond the bell curve." In fact, the most important reason for reforming the schools arises from ethical considerations of what we owe our students.

The fear of being caught in a church-state controversy has often caused educators to aim for neutrality. This, at times, may have gone too far and taken public education away from its ethical base. This trend should be reversed if restructuring of public education is to reach full potential.

Ethical practices encompass the very basis of public education, but they do so without entanglement in religious tenets. However, both the practice and teaching of ethical conduct inhabits common ground with great religions, successful businesses, and many commonly recognized professions.

REFERENCES

1. Thomas J. Sergiovanni, *Moral Leadership: Getting to the Heart of School Improvement*. Jossey-Bass Publications, San Francisco, CA, pg. 29.

2. A. Bloom, *The Closing of the American Mind: How Higher Education Has Failed Democracy and Impoverished Today's Students* (1987). Simon and Schuster, New York, NY.

3. E.D. Hirsch, Jr., *Cultural Literacy: What Every American Needs to Know* (1987). Houghton-Mifflin, Boston, MA.

4. *Ibid.*, pp. 101–102.

5. Diane Ravitch, *The Schools We Deserve: Reflections on the Educational Crises of Our Time* (1985). Basic Books, Harper Collins Publishers, pp. 23–24.

6. *Ibid.*, pg. 103.

7. Hugh Sockett, in *The Moral Dimensions of Teaching*, Chapter 7, pg. 40, John I. Goodlad, Roger Soder, and Kenneth A. Sirotnik. Jossey-Bass, Inc. Publishers, 350 San-

some Street, San Francisco, CA 94104.

8. Edwin Margolis and Stanley Moses, *The Elusive Quest: The Struggle for Equality of Educational Opportunity* (1992). The Apex Press, New York, NY, pg. 120.

7

ADMINISTERING THE RESTRUCTURED ORGANIZATION

INTRODUCTION

Changing the schools involves a broad constituency. Reformers can be committees, school principals, involved parents, central office administrators, superintendents, school board members, and others. However, once forward movement begins, continuing progress is heavily reliant upon administrative skill. This chapter departs from the broad audience addressed in some of the other chapters and focuses on administrators—mostly principals and superintendents.

CHANGE

One might describe the role of administrator as a facilitator of change. To "maintain the status quo" means to "lose ground." This is because the administrator who tries to maintain the organization always has those with a bright new concept chomping at his or her heels. A maintenance view of organization in which the status quo is supported can be seen often in a late-mid-career administrator, one who is 5 to 8 years from retirement. By this time, he or she has many battle scars and is beginning to think, "I just need to hold this organization together for a few more years."

This is when the administrator begins to get into difficulty. He or she quits taking risks. There is a big difference between gambling and risk-taking. Gambling is an activity of chance. One gives up a measure of responsibility with chance whereas a risk involves effort and control. Risk often requires assuming responsibility—putting oneself "on the line" to attempt the best and correct action to move the organization ahead.

Those who are motivated initiate difficulties for the administrator who quits taking risks. They soon become impatient. Rather than leading the organization into new challenges, the senior administrator who has become a comfort seeker expends effort to preserve the status quo. In an organization which values the status quo, energy is spent putting out brush fires rather than creating fires. Aggressive people in lower levels of the organization soon become disenchanted, giving up or becoming a part of an internal opposition which undermines the top leadership.

There is intrinsic value in change, not random or mindless change, but change directed toward commonly identified goals. Once, while consulting, I made the above statement and was confronted by the response, "Change what? I am part of an effective organization, and if we begin to tinker with it, we may mess things up!" I wanted to respond, "You are probably on your way down now." But instead I said, "Even though you value your present effort, I imagine that there are several small areas which you could target for further improvement."

Once while discussing a new learning program in my district, I said, "This is an excellent opportunity—once we get this implemented, we will just about be there." A very senior member of the group responded, "We are always changing! No one is ever satisfied—I just want to ask one question. When in the ____ are we going to get there?" The whole staff was shocked at the emotion seen in this colleague's remark, and I found myself with all eyes and ears, waiting for a response. The response was not difficult; it required just three words: "Quite honestly, never." As Fullan states in his powerful little book about change:

"We must ask at the outset why is it important that education develop such change capacity, or if you like, what is the promise of educational change if it were to get that good? One could respond at the abstract level that change is all around us, the self-renewing society is essential, education must produce critical thinkers and problem solvers, but these have become clichés. A deeper reason. . . . The moral purpose is to make a difference in the lives of students regardless of background and to help produce citizens who can live and work productively in increasingly dynamically complex societies. This is not new either, but what is new, I think, is the realization that to do this puts teachers precisely in the business of continuous innovation and change. They are, in other words, in the business of making improvements, and to make improvements in an ever changing world is to contend with and manage the focus of change on an ongoing basis" (1).

An effective organization must be dynamic. That is, it must be in an evolutionary process. There are two reasons for this: (a) perfection is a goal, but in organizations it will be a continuing goal rather than an accomplishment, and (b) even if the organization is working effectively it must be tended regularly and it must be moving to the next plateau, because it can't remain the same.

This change concept of effective organization comes from the realization that human organizations are always changing whether or not we want them to do so. Organizations are based upon human relationships. Relationships change as the lives and interests of people change. They change with each new person added or with the loss of each person; and as people work together, they often change their respective roles from task to task. They grow at different rates, and if we let the staff member with the knowledge and skill emerge and lead with the appropriate task, another catalyst for change occurs.

The concept of change should not be unsettling. Rather, it should be embraced as a tool for the vitality of the organization. Wheatly aptly said:

> "Our concept of organization is moving away from the mechanistic creations that flourished in the age of bureaucracy. We have begun to speak in interest of more fluid, organic structures, even of boundaryless organizations. We are beginning to recognize organizations as systems, construing them as "learning organizations" and crediting them with some type of self-renewing capacity. These are our first, tentative forays into a new appreciation for organizations. My own experience suggests that we can forgo the despair created by such common events as change. . . ." (2)

One who advocates change as a way of life in educational organizations might be labeled as "willing to throw everything out the window for the sake of doing it." This is far from the truth. Change must be governed by those elements which were previously discussed—a vision and a mission.

Of course, vision is not a steady guide for change because it is also dynamic. However, vision can provide considerable direction for change because organizations often work backward from their vision in order to make it happen.

The best catalyst for change is the mission statement. It changes infrequently, and the mission statement usually sets out the purpose of the organization in a short but gripping statement. Wheatly explains this concept graphically when discussing her thoughts of organization while observing a mountain stream:

> "This stream has an impressive ability to adapt, to shift the configurations, to let the power balance move, to create new structures. But driving this adaptability, making it all happen, I think, is the water's need to flow. Water answers to gravity, to downhill, to the call of the ocean. The form changes, but the mission remains clear. . . ." (3)

FACILITATING CHANGE

The slightest change in an organization creates disequilibrium or discomfort. Avoiding discomfort is not a basic human need, but it serves as a motivator simply because need fulfillment is put into jeopardy if discomfort is created within an organization. Therefore, the path of least resistance may seem to be to simply try to maintain the organization. We have already seen that this course of action—no matter how attractive it may appear—leads to stagnation, disintegration, and ineffectiveness. The appropriate question might be how can change be embraced in an orderly manner?

There are literally dozens of new books about managing change on the market for leaders in both business and education. Each has an approach to working with change that "works" or a story of a transformation which was effective. There is a common factor found in almost all of these works—a quality leadership style which facilitates change and lifts the spirit of those within the organization.

Another commonality which emerges is that the leader is a consensus builder for the mission. As such, he or she is able to lead in a broad based, participatory development of mission with the consensus for change emerging as those who developed the mission try to accomplish its purpose.

The leader or change facilitator should have these qualities:

♦ Be accepting of others—separate assessment of work from assessment of a person (each person remains important, unique, and valuable)

♦ Be a cheerleader for accomplishment—go out of the way to find the positive and give genuine recognition

♦ Be able to keep the vision in the forefront—lead in the developing of a vision and keep it visible

♦ Be a master of communication—make sure that all stakeholders know what is happening and how it relates to the vision and mission

♦ Be a guide for other members of the organization—help them see how change can be need fulfilling

♦ Be a builder of consensus—strive for at least partial closure on the big questions—What's our goal (mission)? Where are we going (outcomes)? What do we need to do to get these outcomes accomplished (planning)?

A very effective way for a school administrator to facilitate change without creating too much disequilibrium is to lead in developing a mission statement, if there is none, and work with the staff on the organizational vision, if there is none. Once these two things are in place, the administrator should lead in forming group consciousness about what actions are needed to facilitate the accomplishment of the mission. Of course, these two tasks may not be the very first tasks in organizational change (see the model in Chapter 3).

This discussion of some concepts of change dovetails nicely with Chapter 1. The ability of the leader to function in a climate of change is critical if education is to move beyond the bell curve. Two important skills that will help in this effort are to identify the "what if" strategy and to use incrementalism in the change process.

THE DEADLY "WHAT IF" STRATEGY

A "what if" question is often used to confound and confuse the issue rather than to seek information. This is a very effective and subtle form of opposition to change, and the leader must recognize this strategy and take steps to counter it, or any new idea will simply be "what if'd" to death.

To counter "what if" activity, divide into study groups which formulate questions in writing, and assign the questions to the appropriate group for research. For example, a high school staff was working on changing from a seven-period day to a four-period day. "What if" questions began immediately. What if we lose accreditation? What if students transfer? What if we create disciplinary problems with a long lunch? What if teachers have difficulty with the longer period?

The principal recognized the problem and immediately asked each person to write possible questions for a research committee.

The committee formulated a single list of questions and assigned them to subcommittees for study and a report to the entire faculty. In this manner, a large number of faculty members became involved. It is noteworthy that a well-known resistor was given the role of formulating the questions into a single document.

INCREMENTALISM

Previous discussion about the importance of a new mission, of vision, and of outcomes may have left the impression that the public schools should be simultaneously reorganized from top to bottom. Even if this were true, it would not be possible. The old mission, the old expectancies, and the status quo would prevent such sweeping change.

The fact that change will be resisted points to the value of having a vision, a mission, and outcomes. If one knows where one is going, it may be necessary to get there in increments. The increments will have purpose and each move will fit the direction like a piece in a giant puzzle.

For example, it might not be possible to identify and outlaw at once every practice in education which is a holdover from the select and sort era, replacing each with a practice supported by research and data as productive for most students. However, it is possible to identify a new mission and to jointly create a vision, then systematically, through staff development, add new practices which will cause a "loss of innocence" about the inappropriateness of outdated, counterproductive practices—this is incrementalism.

MANAGING CONFLICT

A constant in educational leadership focused on change is the management of conflict. The ability to manage conflict is a necessary asset of the successful leader.

I use the term "managing conflict" rather than resolving conflict because resolving implies "resolution." This is the goal, but it may not always be possible. Managing conflict implies working with conflict, possibly to achieve resolution, but at least to reduce enmity.

Managing conflict, then, implies three goals in descending

order—(a) resolution; (b) accommodation; (c) reducing enmity. Reaching resolution or achieving accommodation may be familiar, but reducing enmity may need more discussion. It is an effective strategy for the leader who wants to achieve a reasonable period of tenure in order to give consistent leadership to a school restructuring effort.

Earlier we discussed the problems with leadership turnover, particularly among superintendents. Strategies for maintaining the effort to restructure through a leadership change were explored. Of course, the best way to solve this problem is for the leader to stay. The use of appropriate conflict management strategies such as reducing enmity can help with this effort.

Reducing enmity is taking the emotion from the opposition. It is refusing to allow "righteous" indignation. It is reaching a state where the focus is on the point of concern, rather than the leader. It's true, leadership requires taking a stand, and occasionally an unpopular stand, with very little room for compromise. Whether such occasions result in a "Moriarty complex" on the part of the opposition is often in the hands of the leader.

What is a "Moriarty complex"? It is where an opponent develops such distaste as a result of a disagreement that he or she emerges with a view of the leader as the enemy, and opposes him or her—not the issues. A person with a "Moriarty complex" perceives the leader's motivation on every issue to be threatening. Such a person will seize every chance to attack. Every mistake that the leader might make is exploited and used as a reason for advocating his or her demise.

A leader cannot afford to have many persons with a Moriarty complex because these persons will unite with the opposition on issues for which they have no concern except for the overriding motivation to oppose the leader. An assessment which is useful is that "friends are transient and enemies are permanent." It's true, and when the leader is embroiled in conflict, enemies from the past will emerge and add to the opposition—not only do they add, but they also will attempt to broaden the conflict. They will almost always oppose a negotiated settlement, because the conflict is a valuable vehicle and settlement will take away this vehicle. It is difficult for the leader to deal with this situation. How many times have we heard, "I've made every effort to settle this. . . . I just don't understand where they are coming from." The fact is, at least part of the opposition is coming from past issues. For this group, the only acceptable settlement is the demise of the leader.

The last few paragraphs explained just how important the last option in conflict management is. The following are some strategies for reducing enmity:

♦ Focus the conflict on the issue. If you have ever agreed with this person or group on another issue, exploit it with a comment such as, "We agreed on _____, but on this one we disagree. I feel we can continue to be friends and can agree to disagree." If you have ever disagreed, exploit this also with a statement similar to, "We have disagreed, and if I were not so concerned about this issue I would give up now because you are a formidable opponent. I am sorry we are on different sides but from past experience I know we can remain friends."

♦ Show respect and concern. Find out personal information and good things. Use them to keep the personal side cordial. An example: Suppose you are a superintendent in a board meeting and you know Mrs. Jones is coming in opposition to a grading policy. Find out the grades of her children, any activities in which they are participating, and if she has children in college, etc. When it's time for her to speak introduce her, and, if appropriate, tell the Board about her children, mention the one in college. Start to improve relationships by finding out as much as possible about detractors: hobbies, colleges attended, spouse's name, and common nonconfidential and appropriate things. Many times, this helps to keep the opponent in perspective as a human being. Your interest in them and knowledge about them will be quite disarming. Do all this with the same pleasure as introducing a donator with a $50,000 check.

♦ Find an alternative. This is of value even though it could be unsuccessful. It shows you are trying.

Recently, a very successful teacher planned an out-of-state field trip. The trip was a reward because the class had won special recognition with a class project. However, the trip would cost each student more than $300 and would have taken three other teachers out of the classroom. After the superintendent turned down the field trip, a few of the parents appealed to the school board. The board supported the superintendent's decision. Following board action, the superintendent told the board in open session, "Mr. _____ does excellent work with his class. I can understand his disappointment and that of the class. Because of the purpose to reward the class for a significant project, I would like for us to provide transportation cost for a similar in-state activity."

Of course this solution possibly had little immediate effect, but it showed concern and effort. As a result, the teacher did not become bitter, and even though some of the parents disagreed, they could sense concern. This is much more productive than reprimanding the teacher for planning prior to seeking approval or being upset with the parents for supporting the teacher before the school board. This type of response leads to enmity.

♦ Follow-up with communication. If someone is upset with you, refuse to allow them not to communicate. Follow-up with an expression of concern. Express sorrow about the disagreement, and continue to respond as if the disagreement did not happen. Statements such as, "I know we couldn't agree on the bus change, but we can't afford to lose you as a school supporter," and "We continue to need people like you who care enough to go to bat with a concern." If a positive response is not forthcoming, don't worry. Remember, resolution or accommodation did not work, and the elimination of enmity is the new goal. It's much more difficult for an opponent to maintain enmity if one continues to communicate.

♦ Give credit to a formidable opponent. Once, a teacher opposed a change in the working hours required (15 minutes were added to the day) because the school enrollment had grown, causing problems with lunch and crowd control before and after school. This teacher began to lead the opposition. Finally, she was relegated to the role of gatekeeper. We told her that we respected her opposition, and began to involve her early so she could have all the facts. During the next couple of years, her opposition lost its emotion, and she became objective. She continued to be outspoken, but she became issue-focused rather than opposition-focused. In this role, she became a person whose input was valued.

♦ Avoid personalizing conflict. When we allow ourselves to take conflict personally, we begin to carry the enmity which we are trying to dissuade in others. There is nothing more effective for developing dislike and active distrust than for someone to realize that we do not like them. Occasionally, leaders will perceive that there are some persons who dislike them. We must not respond with actions which project similar feelings.

All of these suggestions are offered as practical ways to defuse the emotion required to develop enmity. Of course, resolution or accommodation are preferred, but reducing enmity is extremely useful. Admittedly, active enemies can accumulate fast for leaders who are creating change. If the strategies outlined here are used, those persons who disagree may simply become opponents rather than enemies.

There are three important strategies which are effective in working with difficult people: (a) expressing empathy, (b) using inquiry, and (c) becoming disarming. There are times when every one of these strategies can be used. They may not solve the problem, but they will usually be very helpful.

One will probably never be involved in a disagreement in which the other person is totally wrong. In expressing *empathy*, give credit for any good points made and let the opposition sense and value their concern. Express empathy with something like, "I know you sensed this plan was unfair because students who did not study the first time would have another chance by taking a retest. You must have thought this particularly unfair for those who worked hard, and did well the first time."

In the use of *inquiry*, the other person can sense your interest. In conversation, say something like, "Let me see if I understand your concern." Repeat the problem, and ask questions such as, "What do you think the outcome of our present policy will be?" and "How do you think we can administer this policy while addressing your concern?" or "What changes do you suggest?" I have used this strategy many times and have seen the other party go through a complete mental examination of the conflict, finally conceding, "I guess that policy is about as good as any when considering all the variables. I guess you just need to be aware of some of the concerns." Of course, this would be resolution, and a result like this is serendipitous, indeed.

A *disarming* strategy is useful in working with argumentative persons. For example, "We made a mistake in initiating this policy. We did not explain the reasons adequately to persons who were most concerned. I can understand why you feel concern." This strategy reduces hostility and, at least, shows you to be conciliatory. It disarms the other person tremendously when you admit to some contributing role in the disagreement.

Some of these concepts were adopted from *The Feeling Good Handbook*, by Dr. David Burns (4). My background is in psychology (prior to educational administration), and this book provided a nice update in an easy-to-follow format.

A very useful concept which Burns discusses is the "I feel"

concept. It's much more productive in a disagreement to tell the opposer "I feel that my point is not being considered here" rather than "You are totally ignoring my point of view," or "I feel badly because I sense my commitment to this is not understood" rather than "I resent your accusing me of not caring." Through the use of this procedure, you can keep the focus on effects and outcomes rather than the other person.

"YOU" STATEMENTS

The most nonproductive thing in a confrontation is to become defensive, but this may also be the most difficult aspect to control. When we become defensive, we are not likely to use the techniques outlined earlier. We are more likely to attack the other person with "you" statements. This leads to deeper conflict and will put us well on the way to developing an enemy. A "you" statement is the opposite of an "I feel" statement. A "you" statement lays the blame squarely on the other person. This usually causes the other person to respond with hostility.

It is important to continue to build competence in working through disputes. Keep the goal in focus and "cut losses" when agreement cannot be reached.

When a principal or superintendent gets into difficulty, the root is usually an inability to conduct interpersonal relations. It has been said often, with "tongue in cheek," that a principal can be practically incompetent but love people and he or she will not be "found out" for 2 or 3 years. Of course, this folklore may not be entirely accurate, but it does place the appropriate emphasis on people skills.

WORKING WITH THE MEDIA

No one gets "good press" all the time. There are, however, some people who get favorable press much of the time, and there are others who seldom get positive press at all. Of course, it seems that there is a national penchant to find and publish bad news about the schools.

A recent experience with a public hearing serves as a typical example of working with the media. A rather large parent group (more than 200) appeared to support the construction of a new school in their attendance zone. In reality, it was a fairly positive hearing. The parents were well-organized, they had their facts straight, and they presented a credible case.

The school board was receptive to input from the parents and agreed to speed up the beginning of construction. Of the three reporters who often covered school board meetings, one attended. The other two were on assignment elsewhere and called me for information the next day.

I have a long-time acquaintance with all three reporters, and any of the three would feel comfortable calling. When the first one called, I said that I was surprised by the size of the group, but that the meeting was a nice exercise of public participation. I explained that the input was well-organized and well-informed, and that the school board was responsive. The reporter's comment was something like, "Well, I didn't miss anything too earthshaking then."

When the second reporter called I said, "I'm glad you called. I want to tell you about the awful meeting—that was a potentially violent crowd—I was fearful for my life!" I actually could hear the excitement in the reporter's voice as he began to ask questions. Of course, I could also sense the disappointment in the "doggone you" when I said I was joking. As mentioned, we were well-acquainted, and the relationship permitted some good humored teasing.

The experience with the second reporter shows the excitement created by bad news or inappropriate behavior. Did the second reporter have the goal of embroiling the schools in controversy? Not at all! But he had a "nose" for the kind of story which would quickly catch the reader's attention.

The problem in working with the media is that there are many attention getting topics provided by the schools, and reporters will report them. The public has a tendency to believe that public schools are centers for crime, violence, and drugs. An occasional negative occurrence can become the expected confirmation. For example, a news story of a student who left home with his father's handgun and brought it to school to show a friend can now create panic for an entire community. This is an almost impossible problem for the school administrator. The school may be well-managed and this may have been the only incident with a handgun. The administrator may have been on top of the problem. However, the incident is going to hurt when published. In most communities, it must be published to avoid possible charges of a "cover up," at the least. The press can give the story a sympathetic spin with a simple quote like, "The school administrators acted quickly." This is one reason it is important to cultivate positive relationships. The following procedures are helpful in working with the media:

♦ Always be truthful—Work on building credibility. Frank, honest, and complete answers to reporter's questions are a must.

♦ Prepare in advance—Anticipate questions. Have only one spokesperson. For example, in the gun incident it is reasonable to assume the news will leak from the school, or the media will get the police report if either the gun or student were turned over to the police. Prepare to answer questions in advance. In fact, some administrators prefer to initiate media contact themselves.

♦ Give previously prepared briefing sheets on anticipated topics to the media prior to covered meetings. For example, if a topic on the agenda is *Providing Free Textbooks*, the briefing paper should include cost, reasons, problems, and other information.

♦ Welcome the media to official meetings. For example, make sure that they have seats with places to write, and lay out material. If coffee is available, make sure they are invited to help themselves.

♦ When organizing official meetings, accommodate the media. Consider deadlines and avoid executive sessions which force members of the media to stand around waiting. School boards can hold necessary executive sessions either before the meeting starts or after the regular agenda is finished.

♦ Do not confront the members of the media. This doesn't mean that biased or incorrect coverage should go unnoted, but point out the problem as if the reporter were a colleague seeking to do an effective job. Most of the time, this is the case! Unless the reporter has, through your defensiveness, become the opposition, a good humored "you got us this time" with a casual correction is usually well-received. You probably won't get a retraction, but, perhaps, greater care next time. As the change process is attempted, there will be occasions when working with the media will be important. Begin change with a communication strategy such as that mentioned in Chapter 2 and incorporate the suggestions above.

PERSONAL PRODUCTIVITY

The administrator who is also a leader, can change the organization through resource allocation, planning, and vision. Nanus (5) made a similar observation:

"As a leader, you are likely to have the skills and authority to both directly and indirectly steer the changes. Directly you have the authority to make the key decisions on resource allocations, staffing, structure, information flows, and operating processes that determine what shall and what shall not be done by the organization. Indirectly, you can influence the behavior of others and orient them toward the new destination through consultation, participation, persuasion, inspiration, and rewards. In addition, you can set up special task forces charged with specific implementation responsibilities.

"Both directly and indirectly, you can work to develop strategic thinking supportive of your vision and alter the organizational climate to make the vision's attainment more likely."

Personal productivity is necessary for the administrator who would change the vision of an organization. In order to have time to accomplish all the things needed, the leader needs an abundance of personal productivity tools.

GETTING CONTROL OF TIME

Without a plan for controlling time, the administrator may walk into the office in the morning and exit at night wondering where the time went. This can happen day after day. The administrator becomes boxed in, and communication is restricted to those who come to the office or call. Meetings are viewed as lengthy intrusions which take time away from desk work involving an endless web of red tape.

The foregoing paragraph may be a slightly exaggerated or overstated problem, but time management is a problem which affects educational administrators to a considerable extent. It is true—routine tasks and interruptions can take the time available from the important functions of attending the vision, leading the instructional program and spending time with colleagues. Some of the following ideas may be helpful:

- List four things to accomplish each day. Write them on a card or a computer. If one of them is not accomplished, give it first priority the next day.

- Divide each day and week into segments. Every day, include time for paperwork, time to be out of the office, and time for appointments, call-backs, planning, and miscellaneous activities. During each week, hold out one day to visit personnel and other constituents. "Call-backs" are the time spent returning calls. If an effort is made to avoid interruptions, then call-backs are a must.

- Plan short breaks in the busy schedule. For example, take a few minutes a couple of times each day to get a cup of coffee or whatever. On the way to and from the coffee pot, try to spend a minute or two with a few coworkers. This builds relationships and is relaxing.

- Be wary of organizers such as computer calendars, note-taking devices, cellular phones, etc. Technology can be wonderful, but it can also add to one's burden. For example, a friend shared that use of a computer actually slowed his progress. He was a slow typist, and would invariably spend time learning new software. He decided that he was wasting time in front of the screen. He finally limited his use of the computer to spreadsheets for budgeting projections and salary scales. He would ask his secretary to set up many of the things he wanted for work.

♦ Plan meetings in advance. For short meetings, a few notes will suffice. For more lengthy staff meetings, have an agenda, and share it with all attenders in advance.

♦ Start meetings on time and end on time. This demonstrates regard for those in attendance, and it demonstrates a regard for time and operating in a businesslike fashion. When meetings begin 10 or 15 minutes late, lateness among attenders is encouraged. If meetings are always started on time (even if there is only one person in attendance) lateness of attenders soon ends and punctuality becomes the norm.

The Sponge Activity—A 5-minute "sponge" activity to start the meeting on time is very useful. I learned this method years ago while watching Madeline Hunter work with a group of teachers. She was talking about transitions where children enter the class, either at the beginning of the day or from some activity such as physical education. The sponge activity was a brief activity designed to focus the attention of children as they settled down, and to set the stage for the ensuing activity. A sponge activity was not a new skill, it was just a neat focusing activity or review that eliminated the waste of time while the children were coming into class.

A sponge activity also is an excellent way to

begin administrative staff meetings. It enables the meeting to begin on time, and for those who might drift in, there would not have to be any "catching up." It's interesting that the same persons are usually late, and when they find that the meeting is underway with no review, they begin to arrive on time.

Administrative sponge activities also are things which are interesting and informative, but not critical. Some examples are:

- A report from the committee working on salary and fringe benefit recommendations for the administrative staff.

- An update on something recently in the headlines. For example, what really happened with the "gun" incident, and what were the plans for working with the media, teachers, and other constituents?

- Give out and discuss a short research article and discuss the local implications it might have.

- Call on someone to relate a humorous story which occurred while an administrative team was visiting another school system.

For sponge activities, the late arriver need not participate. It is helpful if the sponge activity is of sufficient interest that those not on time regret missing a part of the discussion.

♦ Delegate—The ability to delegate is one of the most essential productivity tools of the successful administrator. There are two primary kinds of problem behaviors related to delegation: (a) the executive who will not let go when he or she delegates, and (b) the executive who delegates well, but fails to follow-up properly.

The primary skill in "letting go" involves getting out of the way once you delegate a task. Often one wants to "spoon-feed" after delegation:

giving information in bits and pieces, continuing to be involved in the project which has been delegated, or changing and reworking the project once it is completed. All are control tactics.

Continuing to be involved in the delegated project takes several important things out of the process of delegating. First, it takes time which kills the value of delegating. Second, it does not allow the delegatee to develop the self-confidence needed to independently complete projects. The best practice is to literally force coworkers to independently complete delegated work. "Force" sounds coercive, but this is not intended. Force simply means to use the following two skills:

- Set an appropriate "time due" for each delegated project and write it on your calendar. Set a follow-up time a few days in advance of the time due. On the follow-up date, ask how things are going. Refer the worker to any help necessary, but avoid assuming any part in the project.

- When persons with delegated tasks come to you for assistance, avoid giving concrete answers or getting involved. Rather, help the colleague to visualize solutions through questioning techniques, and then encourage them to continue and come up with the final recommendation.

It is very common for colleagues who have been assigned projects to attempt inadvertently to pull the delegator into the decisionmaking process. Avoid this by helping them clarify the issue through a nondirective discussion. Keep them in the decisionmaking mode. This helps coworkers build self-confidence.

The Administrator's Guide to Personal Productivity by Harold Taylor gives much more depth and consideration to the issues involved in organizing tasks for productivity. This resource is an excellent guide for group study on mission setting, goal setting, running an office efficiently, delegation, stress, etc. (6)

Many of the things which consume the most time are important, and they cannot be neglected, but they are not really what our job is all about. If we handle them efficiently, there will be time to think and plan, and to work on moving the organization forward through promoting the achievement of the mission, selling the vision, and monitoring outcomes.

WORKING WITH THE BUREAUCRACY

Outstanding principals manage to operate an excellent school despite limiting factors. This is the consistent factor in much of the school effectiveness literature. At any level, there are few "stars" who perform despite limiting factors. They appear to understand certain skills and work techniques that overcome bureaucratic banners. However, many educators including teachers, assistant principals, principals, central administrators, and even school board members accept limitations created by another level of the bureaucracy. One should avoid using other organizations or persons as an excuse for not moving the schools in a forward direction.

We will discuss various levels of bureaucracy which impact education. The following are some suggestions for leaders working effectively within the constraints posed by these organizations.

The astute administrator keeps an ear to the ground for the next "in thing," but avoids the tendency to jump from innovation to innovation. If the organization has a direction guided by a vision, mission, and outcomes, it can incorporate new programs and research related to this established direction. The critical thing is to keep the direction. Often this is difficult because the direction at the state level seems to change with each election.

STATE DEPARTMENTS OF EDUCATION

It is the exceptional state department of education that can effectively lead in an educational restructuring movement. The favored tool of most states is the mandate. When those at the state level try to force change over an entire state, the mandates may stifle the best school systems and confound those needing the most help.

With funding power, the state is able to impose change, but typically of the component nature. Contextual change often escapes consideration. Of course, the results are tinkering and superficial changes.

A wonderful characteristic of public education is resilience. This resilience enables education to withstand the onslaught of special interests which would pull the public schools in a million different directions. This same resilience makes top-down change very difficult.

The goal of the state should be to employ an outstanding staff and conduct training and consultation on the "cutting edge." Often, politicians legislate uninformed solutions and occupy the attention and energies of state educational personnel. To insulate the department from political pressure, research-based training and development should be conducted by those two or three levels down from top state leadership.

Politics also result in a flood of mixed messages from the state that keeps local educators in a struggle. For example, currently there is a thrust for high academic standards. This advocacy for standards results in positions which resemble the "back to basics" movement, often spearheaded by persons aligned with the business community. Simultaneously, many business leaders are ranking the following skills as critical:

♦ The ability to work with others
♦ The ability to adjust to change
♦ Steady work ethics
♦ The ability to use technology
♦ The ability to solve problems and think creatively

Some state departments that have developed learner outcomes based on the above list have then backed down when accused of promoting the teaching of values and spongy "feel good concepts." This leaves local school systems without the assistance and leadership which the state could provide. This quandary happens because two different directions are being advocated simultaneously, sometimes by members of the same group.

The advice which results from this discussion of the state bureaucracy and the problems with top-down leadership is:

♦ Don't rely on state mandates as a basis for school change. Mandates must be attended to, but there is no substitute for local effort.

♦ Continue a program of building grass roots consciousness for the needed changes in education.

♦ Use state mandates and parameters of state law and regulations as a backdrop while developing productive changes within the organization.

LOCAL SCHOOL BOARDS

Local school boards can assist and hinder reform of public education. I know of no other body quite like a local school board. For example, where in the business world would one find a $100,000,000 business whose board of directors includes a waitress, a realtor, a college professor and a homemaker? Of course, the occupations above are all respected, but they illustrate the diversity of many local boards of education.

For many school boards, the size and complexity of the organization is simply beyond the comprehension permitted by the members previous preparation. On the plus side, local boards are almost overwhelmingly supportive of quality education. The down side is that in their zeal to contribute, they often lapse into micromanagement. A board member may not understand organizational theory or the broad consequences of policy issues, so he will sink his teeth into the lunch menu of the neighborhood elementary school or Susie's stolen tennis shoes.

As a result of micromanagement, the local superintendent incurs an extra burden of answering endless questions about small problems that have been brought to board members by constituents. The superintendent may find that the board member has already committed to a solution, thus undermining the superintendent's leadership ability. It's difficult for a "toothless tiger" to provide the leadership needed for a school system.

School boards are usually elected and political pressure of various types affects policy. Ideally, school board service should be an end in itself, focused on providing the best education possible for the students. Unfortunately, school board members begin to consider reelection or higher elective office and encounter numerous groups with various ideas of what constitutes "the best education possible."

The "best education possible" for some may be to send a high school band to the Rose Bowl Parade while reducing funds for science instructional materials. This type of decision-making is disconcerting for an administrator. It's somewhat like playing "watch the bouncing ball," while the ball stops at pressure points for decisionmaking. This is, perhaps, the main problem with local school boards.

A competent administrator will want the school board to stick with policymaking and stay clear of day-to-day administrative decisions. The administrator will also want the school board to make provisions to insulate itself from political pressure as much as possible, and make decisions on the basis of research and data.

Most school boards and superintendents work out a loose accommodation. The superintendent seeks to make the board appear in a positive light, and the school board attempts to stay away from micromanagement of the school system. When this arrangement works, it provides enough security for administrators to accomplish their work.

When the system breaks down, the board and the superintendent must use patience and negotiating skills to get back on track. If negotiations do not succeed, both sides may become polarized. The result is a tug-of-war, and the morale of the entire organization begins to erode. Ultimately, educational progress is disrupted, and the superintendent leaves.

Following are actions to enhance cooperation between the school board and the superintendent:

For the Superintendent

♦ Communicate with the board.
  • Furnish analysis of key issues in the form of an occasional one page summary.
  • Try to visit each school board member no less than bi-monthly—this can be formal or

informal. I know a superintendent who hand delivers the agenda to each board member.

- Don't expect policy changes immediately after suggestions are brought to the table; allow 1 month, if possible.

♦ Be willing to compromise—try to restructure a difficult problem so that the solution is one both parties can live with.

♦ Bring several positive reports to each board meeting.
  - Ask the responsible staff members to report.
  - Have information prepared for the media.
  - Include teachers as much as possible.

♦ When a position or a point of advocacy is lost, move on—don't gripe to outsiders.

♦ Take the long-term view.
  - Have back-up positions.
  - Present the board with two acceptable alternatives which will be consistent with long-term goals, when possible.

For the Board

♦ Avoid putting the superintendent in a bad light publicly.
  - Don't give casual consideration to his or her recommendations and then discuss other alternatives in more depth.
  - If the superintendent's recommendations are off-base, explain the problems and either defer a decision until the superintendent can offer a compromised recommendation or furnish additional information.

♦ Don't make promises to constituents on an issue prior to hearing the superintendent's recommendation.

♦ Avoid conducting your own investigation. Convey concern to the superintendent and ask for a report. Board member investigations bring into question the reliability of the superintendent. If the board can't rely on the superintendent's honesty and integrity, take appropriate steps, but avoid compromising the superintendent by careless behavior.

♦ Discuss the superintendent's performance at least yearly Include the areas of competence noticed and at least one area of needed improvement. Make this procedure standard policy, so the superintendent knows what to expect.

♦ Avoid expecting special favors from the superintendent.

  • Don't take problems from constituents to the superintendent or the principal. Make the constituents do their own communication (through appropriate channels). The "errand runner" is not an appropriate role for a school board member.

  • Avoid requesting inside information in order to appear informed. This may violate confidentiality and cause problems for the superintendent with other board members.

When the school board and superintendent work together cooperatively, the individual school unit can move forward at full speed. Of course, school reform occurs at the local school level. It cannot be mandated effectively from above, but it can be supported and encouraged by conditions set by the local board and superintendent.

THE FEDERAL GOVERNMENT

Occasionally, the Federal Government mandates a program or law which has considerable impact. Head Start is an example of a positive program. Chapter 1 is an example of a program which had high potential but killed much of the innovation it should have supported with rules and regulations.

During the last decade, the role and impact of the Department of Education often has decreased because the politically appointed secretary chose to alienate a substantial portion of the education community by vacillating between demeaning rhetoric and questionable interpretation of research. All this was designed to promote choice by undermining public education. What an outstanding example of how *not* to be successful at motivating educational reform.

SELLING

A successful school administrator must devote much effort to selling. "Success builds upon success," to borrow a statement from the outcome-based proponents. An effective administrator sells the organization, the organization's direction, its individual successes, its ethical values, and, of course, its vision. Some of the following are selling opportunities:

- ◆ Internal Selling—Report positive things about the organization to employees. Use a small portion of each meeting to promote the organization's vision and to build pride in successful activities and occurrences. Every group is important, including bus drivers, instruction assistants, cafeteria workers, substitute teachers, and custodians. Representatives from these groups span the community. Think how persuasive members of all these groups can be if they believe the organization has a direction and is successful in its purpose.

- ◆ External Selling—Sell the organization to everyone who will listen. This includes salesmen and vendors who call on the schools and others with broad contacts. For example, several years ago, I realized many of the community's modest income employees had insurance "Debit Salespersons" who called on them monthly to collect the premium. There were about five such salespersons who covered the entire community, and they were the most educated people with whom many families had continuing contact. Due to this, they asked the salesperson many questions and for opinions. The salespersons were invited for a breakfast session at one of the schools during which we informed them about the most successful programs in the schools. These meetings continued until the "debit salespersons" were phased out by changes in businesses.

External selling includes newsletters, news stories, positive sports reports on the TV cable, and letters to parents highlighting some pertinent aspect of schooling. Local community activities can provide opportunities for selling. For example, two floats participating in a Christmas parade sponsored by the Retail Merchants Association—a school bus with safety patrol members and bus safety slogans and an anti-drug float. Each provided important messages, helped the students through productive projects, and cast the schools in a positive light.

SUMMARY

Restructuring the schools is, to a large extent, a local effort, and local administrators—primarily principals and superintendents—will invariably encounter challenges to their leadership. Being able to navigate these challenges is often the difference between the successful and the unsuccessful.

I have offered concepts proven useful for administrative success. It is the skillful leader who can prevent disequilibrium from disabling the change process.

REFERENCES

1. Michael Fullan, *Change Forces: Probing The Depths of Educational Reform* (1993). The Falmer Press, Taylor and Francis, Inc., 1900 Frost Road, Suite 101, Bristol, PA 19007, pg. 4.

2. Margaret J. Wheatly, *Leadership and the New Science: Learning About Organization from an Orderly Universe.* Barrett-Koehler Publications, San Francisco, CA, pg. 13.

3. *Ibid.*, pg. 16.

4. Dr. David Burns, M.D., *The Feeling Good Handbook* (1989). William Morrow and Company, Inc., 1350 Avenue of the Americas, New York, NY 10019, pp. 421–463.

5. Burt Nanus, *Visionary Leadership* (1992). Jossey-Bass Publishers, 350 Sansome Street, San Francisco, CA 94104, pg. 142.

6. Harold Taylor, *The Administrators Guide to Personal Productivity* (1993). Eye On Education, Inc., Box 388, Princeton, NJ 08550.

8

Moving Beyond the Bell Curve Through Restructuring

A Model for Organizing Change

In this book, we discussed many of the major concepts needed to transform a public educational system, or even a single school, into a place of learning for all students. This brief, final chapter will address how we proceed to change the schools.

I have stressed throughout that change can't be mandated. The folly of attempting to mandate change is apparent at the national, state, and local levels. The only approach which will work is to involve our colleagues in creating a new kind of organization with a supporting vision, mission, and outcomes. This will result in a new paradigm for the business of education.

Admittedly, a change of this magnitude will be the most challenging project one ever attempts. The old paradigm, the select and sort model, has been around for almost 100 years. It permeates our present structure, dominating grading philosophy, grouping practices, teacher evaluation, and even expectancies for achievement. If a paradigm is a way to view reality, then the select and sort model has produced a distorted view which prohibits productivity. In discussing this, Glasser said:

"After twenty years of unsuccessful struggle, all we have accumulated is a pile of evidence that our traditional boss-managed system has taken schools as far as it can. If we do not change from bossing to leading, the schools will not change by any standard" (1).

Change is difficult, but if efforts are based on a plan, and if change can be approached as a long-term project requiring persistence and determination, progress can be made.

In the following pages, I offer a model for organizing change (Figs. 8.1–8.3). In it, I revisit many of the actions which will contribute to change.

Many questions will arise as one considers this 3-year plan. It is a draft of concepts needed for collaboratively developing a school restructuring model. The value of developing a model is that it becomes the plan. Once the decision is made to move beyond the bell curve to a new model for learning, it is extremely important to chart the course of change in advance.

In year one, as members of the study group become familiar with the various knowledge bases, they can assist in developing an instructional model. Members of each subsequent study group should become expert in using this model and should be able to demonstrate its use to other group members. Those who serve as coordinators of new study groups should be able to demonstrate the instructional model in their classrooms.

Questions might arise regarding this model, including why were these particular knowledge bases chosen, why teacher evaluation was listed for revision, how mini-courses are organized, why site-based management is listed, why curriculum alignment is important, how the belief system relates to the credibility task force, and, finally, what is a definition of the job of the peer coach. The following is a brief response to these possible questions.

First, let's discuss the model for action in general. The model offered is for a 3-year plan. This is probably overly optimistic. All the work advocated will possibly take 5 to 7 years for most school systems. Perhaps, the 3-year schedule is reasonable for the single school.

FIGURE 8.1 A MODEL FOR ACTION—YEAR ONE

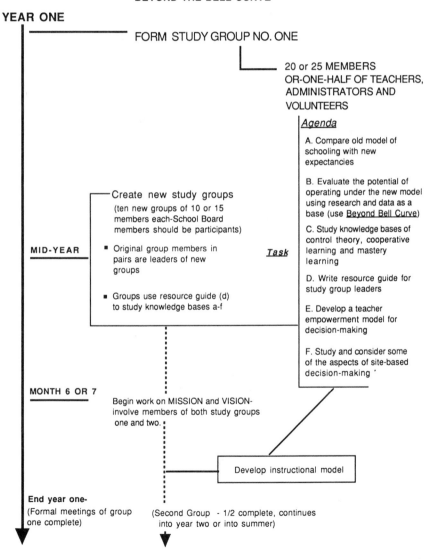

A MODEL FOR ACTION
BEYOND THE BELL CURVE

YEAR ONE

FORM STUDY GROUP NO. ONE

20 or 25 MEMBERS
OR-ONE-HALF OF TEACHERS,
ADMINISTRATORS AND
VOLUNTEERS

Agenda

A. Compare old model of schooling with new expectancies

B. Evaluate the potential of operating under the new model using research and data as a base (use Beyond Bell Curve)

Create new study groups
(ten new groups of 10 or 15 members each-School Board members should be participants)

C. Study knowledge bases of control theory, cooperative learning and mastery learning

MID-YEAR

■ Original group members in pairs are leaders of new groups

Task

D. Write resource guide for study group leaders

■ Groups use resource guide (d) to study knowledge bases a-f

E. Develop a teacher empowerment model for decision-making

F. Study and consider some of the aspects of site-based decision-making '

MONTH 6 OR 7

Begin work on MISSION and VISION-involve members of both study groups one and two.

Develop instructional model

End year one-
(Formal meetings of group one complete)

(Second Group - 1/2 complete, continues into year two or into summer)

FIGURE 8.2 A MODEL FOR ACTION—YEAR TWO

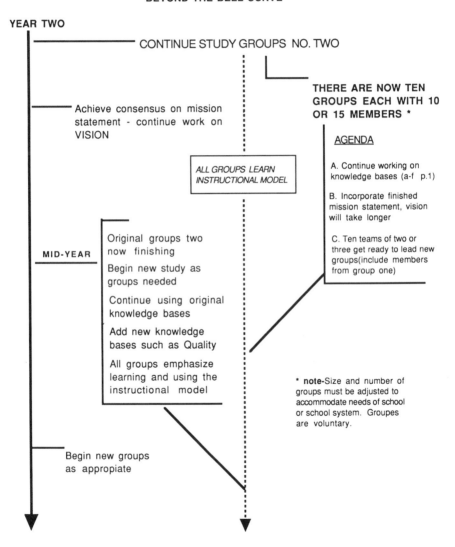

A MODEL FOR ACTION

BEYOND THE BELL CURVE

YEAR TWO

CONTINUE STUDY GROUPS NO. TWO

THERE ARE NOW TEN GROUPS EACH WITH 10 OR 15 MEMBERS *

Achieve consensus on mission statement - continue work on VISION

<u>AGENDA</u>

ALL GROUPS LEARN INSTRUCTIONAL MODEL

A. Continue working on knowledge bases (a-f p.1)

B. Incorporate finished mission statement, vision will take longer

MID-YEAR

Original groups two now finishing

Begin new study as groups needed

Continue using original knowledge bases

Add new knowledge bases such as Quality

All groups emphasize learning and using the instructional model

C. Ten teams of two or three get ready to lead new groups(include members from group one)

***note-**Size and number of groups must be adjusted to accommodate needs of school or school system. Groupes are voluntary.

Begin new groups as appropiate

FIGURE 8.3 A MODEL FOR ACTION—YEAR THREE

A MODEL FOR ACTION
BEYOND THE BELL CURVE

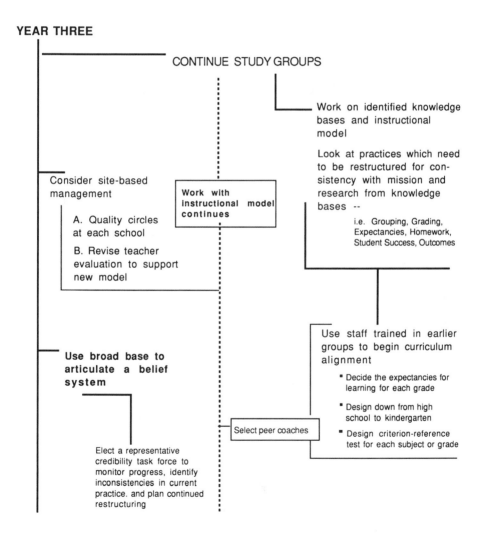

YEAR THREE

CONTINUE STUDY GROUPS

Work on identified knowledge bases and instructional model

Look at practices which need to be restructured for consistency with mission and research from knowledge bases --

  i.e. Grouping, Grading, Expectancies, Homework, Student Success, Outcomes

Consider site-based management

Work with instructional model continues

A. Quality circles at each school

B. Revise teacher evaluation to support new model

Use staff trained in earlier groups to begin curriculum alignment

  * Decide the expectancies for learning for each grade

  * Design down from high school to kindergarten

  * Design criterion-reference test for each subject or grade

Use broad base to articulate a belief system

Select peer coaches

Elect a representative credibility task force to monitor progress, identify inconsistencies in current practice. and plan continued restructuring

There is no guarantee that the model will result in change, because change is complicated and results are unpredictable. Efforts at "easy change" through mandates are ineffective. Fullan outlines the difficulty of the process as follows:

> ". . . Change is a never ending proposition under conditions of dynamic complexity. Another reason that you can't mandate what matters is that you don't know what is going to matter until you are into the journey. If change involved implementing single, well-developed, proven innovations one at a time, perhaps, it could be blueprinted. But school districts are in the business of implementing a bewildering array of multiple innovations and policies simultaneously. . . ." (2)

It is important, however, to begin the journey of change, and the model which is offered gives structure. Of course, there will be problems along the way, but collaboratively finding solutions will provide a catalyst for further progress.

In the model, visioning is a continuing and long-term project while the group completes the mission early. One shouldn't begin work on either until some common knowledge base is gained. Fullan also recognizes that skills, clarity, learning, and new beliefs come first:

> "'Ready, fire, aim' is a more fruitful sequence if we want to take a linear snapshot of an organization undergoing major reform. Ready is important, and there has to be some notion of direction, but it is killing to bog down the process with vision, mission, and strategic planning, before you know enough about dynamic reality. Fire is action and inquiry where skills, clarity, and learning are fostered. Aim is crystallizing new belief, formulating mission and vision statements, and focusing strategic planning. Vision and strategic planning come later; if anything they come at *step 3*—not step 1" (3).

The knowledge bases which are listed in the model were chosen because they represent work which is clearly associated with the concept of "learning for all students."

Once the mission is articulated, everything else—the

instructional model, curriculum alignment, the work of peer coaches, criterion referenced assessment, etc.—relates in a significant way. The mission becomes the statement of shared purpose. It even becomes the basis for continuing to build a new culture, a requirement if change is going to "stick."

The development of mini-courses is an excellent way for study group members to work on various knowledge bases. In most states, recertification points can be given for completion of mini-courses. Two or more mini-courses can be combined for a larger number of credit hours required in other states. For example, a mini-course of 16 or more hours might give one certificate renewal credit, or a combination might provide enough for three certification credits. Often teachers are motivated when the continuing education relates to both certification and change at the local level. Of course, when offering mini-courses, or any training in the knowledge bases, a consultant could be an asset.

Note that midway through year one, new study groups are formed. Members of the original study group should become the coordinators or facilitators of the second round of groups, allowing them to use new knowledge in a positive way. It also gives the work credibility when peers are working together.

The resource guide developed by members of the original group will provide a consistent direction for future groups. New group leaders will have to be ready to lead in just half a year. Two points important to note are: (a) This makes this model move very fast—it may be that the task outlined in the model cannot move at this pace, and (b) ff study groups are created after half a year, the leaders will be involved in two groups simultaneously—this may be too taxing when combined with normal teaching responsibility. Therefore, adjust the time frame to suit local needs.

Several months into the model, groups begin work on the mission and vision. Consensus on mission should be reached early in year two. Work on vision continues slowly, possibly into year three.

Note on the center line that an *instructional model* is developed. An instructional model is an outline of a procedure used in teaching, designed to align practice with the mission.

The instructional model will be invaluable in accomplishing the mission and for guiding the work of the peer coaches. I offer a prototype later, but I do not advocate that a school or school system necessarily adopt my model. Since there is value in building ownership, I suggest in year one that a school team develop an instructional model.

Observe that it is well into the first year that I recommend the development of an instructional model, and even this may be too soon. Planners should have an understanding of the knowledge bases listed prior to developing an instructional model.

Developing an instructional model is one of the most important activities of year one. This is simply the answer to, "How do we get what we want instructionally?" An instructional model does not dictate teaching styles or curriculum. It is a method used to present instructional content. The instructional model includes the components of teaching which the group members agree should be incorporated into most teaching efforts, such as some of the research-based information on effective instructional practices that has surfaced within the last few years. It also includes procedures to assess what students already know and to ensure that most students either know the material or engage in remedial activities prior to summative assessment. Figure 8.4 is an example:

FIGURE 8.4 AN INSTRUCTIONAL MODEL

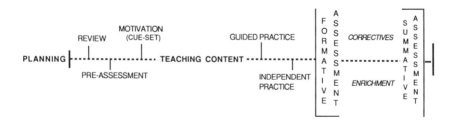

Year three is the time to begin refining the change model,

and to begin seeking credibility. Teachers will take a significant step, as they begin to evaluate instructional practices such as grouping, grading, expectancies, homework, success, and outcomes in terms of consistency with the mission and in light of research and data.

During the third year, several other significant actions should occur. The following three are among the most important:

♦ Articulating a belief system

♦ Beginning curriculum alignment

♦ Selecting peer coaches

The Belief System—This is a statement about the beliefs of the staff of the school system, created by involving the broadest possible constituency. The belief system will have value as a credibility check. For example, every practice within a school or school system should be tested against the belief system.

Beginning Curriculum Alignment—A significant way to achieve quality in the curriculum is to align the curriculum. This task should be begun at the exit point of schooling and the design or alignment should be accomplished backward until reaching a students' level of introduction. There are several advantages to having an aligned curriculum:

♦ Exit skills are identified

♦ Each teacher knows what was taught earlier, what should be taught, and what will be taught next year

♦ One can locate gaps in the curriculum

♦ Educators agree upon curriculum, and the problems with disjointed, haphazard curricula are diminished

Curriculum alignment can be seen as a vehicle for test improvement. This simply means that while the curriculum is being aligned back through the levels, it is also coordinated with any test students must take. A booklet by Fenwick W. English (4) provides excellent guidance for curriculum alignment. English also provides interesting observations about some problems with applying the bell curve to education.

To consider testing in the alignment process may also help prevent a decline in test scores as schools are restructured. As schools are moved away from the select and sort model, the scores on norm referenced tests which support this obsolete model might go down. Curriculum alignment which includes a match between content and test will evade this possibility.

We have discussed testing very briefly in this book. This is because accountability reminds us of the politician who would fix education with various schemes to coerce the unproductive. The folly of this approach to motivation was discussed earlier. Testing is critical, however, as we must know how our students are doing and changing our schools must include a measurement component. We must always strive to answer positively the question—"Are our students becoming successful learners?"

Peer Coaches—A somewhat costly, but productive factor in the change process is the peer coach. Peer coaches are selected from those who have completed the study group training processes. They understand change processes, know the knowledge bases, can demonstrate the instructional model, work with other teachers in a collegial manner, and can help with formatively evaluating teachers.

A peer coaching model might have the following components:

♦ Released time for the peer coach

♦ A limited term for each peer coach (1 year is favored)

♦ A training component—with meetings at least once a month

A peer coach model has a valuable perk. Teachers who are selected as peer coaches enjoy additional contact with peers, and they can improve their own teaching while helping others.

The model for action can continue for several years until every teacher has been involved in a study group. Literally dozens of teachers will have had a chance to lead study groups. As competence in leadership is developed, teachers also have opportunities to present to visitors from other school systems and to present information about restructuring and the change process in other school systems. This is an excellent tool for recognition, and serves to strengthen commitment.

Change is a continuing process, and even if every teacher has been through the training process, there will always be new knowledge bases to learn and new teachers to the system. Therefore, training and study are ongoing.

To move beyond the bell curve and its accompanying select and sort model is a challenging and rewarding journey. The new system which must be created will offer new opportunities for a tremendous number of students who would not have a very good chance for success with the existing system. Best wishes to all who join in this journey for success!

REFERENCES

1. William Glasser, *The Quality School Teacher*. Harper Collins Publishers, Inc., 10 East 53rd Street, New York, NY 10022, pg. 6.

2. Michael Fullan, *Change Forces: Probing the Depths of Educational Reform* (1993). The Falmer Press, Taylor and Francis, Inc., 1900 Frost Road, Suite 101, Bristol, PA 19007, pg. 4.

3. *Ibid.*, pg. 31.

4. Gloria G. Frazier and Robert J. Sickles, *The Directory of Innovations in High Schools* (1993). Eye on Education, Box 388, Princeton Junction, NJ 08550, pg. 136.

5. Fenwick W. English, *Deciding What to Teach and Test* (1992). Corwin Press, Inc., A Sage Publications Company, 2455 Teller Road, Newbury Park, CA 91320, pp. 7–9.

APPENDIX

ORANGE COUNTY PUBLIC SCHOOLS
BELIEF SYSTEM

To accomplish the goals of the organization, individuals assume a role of leadership to promote, guide, and facilitate activities within each school, and the school division as a whole. These individuals include school board members, central office personnel, principals, teachers, and students.

WE BELIEVE THAT EFFECTIVE LEADERS . . .

1. Foster open and accurate communication in a climate of trust.

2. Primarily focus on teaching and learning.

3. Are life-long learners and pursue opportunities for professional growth.

4. Are actively involved in the programs under their direction.

5. Actively seek and provide for appropriate resources.

6. Respect and support their staff.

7. Assure that behaviors are aligned with district beliefs.

8. Build a vision and create the conditions for the vision to become reality.

9. Actively seek assessment of their performance.

10. Strive to make schools safe, inviting places for the entire school community.

11. Use valid, reliable research and involve others in making

decisions.

12.   Share their knowledge and expertise.

13.   Promote a child-centered program.

14.   Recognize that student success is measured by a variety of means.

WE BELIEVE THAT ALL STUDENTS . . .

1.   Desire success and are capable of learning.

2.   Learn best in a safe, positive, and inviting school environment.

3.   Learn at different rates and have different learning styles.

4.   Learn best when taught at the appropriate instructional and developmental levels.

5.   Demonstrate mastery in a variety of ways.

6.   Learn best if they understand the value and purpose of learning.

7.   Are more successful when they actively participate in learning.

8.   Enrich their learning by participation in school and community activities.

9.   Learn best if given frequent feedback and opportunities for self-assessment.

10.   Learn best when they are confident and have a sense of self-worth.

11.   Are more successful when parents value education and share in the responsibility for learning.

12.   Are more successful when they take responsibility for their own actions.

13.   Have various talents, skills, and experiences which affect their learning.

WE BELIEVE THAT EFFECTIVE TEACHERS . . .

1.   Are the key to quality instruction.

2.   Are knowledgeable in their subject areas.

3.   Are organized and skilled in classroom management.

4.   Regularly assess their classroom practices.

5.   Model the behaviors and attitudes they expect of their students.

6.   Establish professional rapport and work cooperatively with others in the best interest of the school and students.

7.   Are life-long learners and pursue opportunities for professional growth.

8.   Communicate with students, parents, administrators, and community in a positive manner.

9.   Demonstrate instructional competency based on valid, reliable research.

10.   Plan and use a variety of instructional strategies to accommodate different learning rates and styles.

11.   Educate students to be responsible citizens.

12.   Foster creativity.

DATE DUE

DEC 3 0 1997			
NOV 2 1 '01			
GAYLORD			PRINTED IN U.S.A.